EDIBLE WILD PLANTS
A GUIDE TO COLLECTING
AND COOKING

by
Ellen Elliott Weatherbee
and
James Garnett Bruce

All rights reserved

© 1982, Ellen Elliott Weatherbee and James Garnett Bruce

Library of Congress Catalog Number: 82-50821

First edition, entitled *Edible Wild Plants of the Great Lakes Region*
    1st printing, 1979
    2nd printing, 1981

Second edition, entitled *Edible Wild Plants A Guide to Collecting and Cooking*
    1st printing, 1982

Cover photograph reprinted with permission from the Macmillan Co. New York, N.Y. copyright © 1979, Peter B. Kaufman and J. Donald LaCroix, *Plants, People, and Environment* p. 359.

Dedicated to the students in our adult education classes at the University of Michigan, and especially to Bob Anderson and Ed Rutz.

And thanks to Janice Glimn Lacy for the drawings, to Carol Mitchell for the advice, to Larry Mellichamp for the picture of the *Menispermum* seed, to Helen Johnson for the photograph on the back cover, and to Helen V. Smith for advice, help, encouragement, and her time.

EDIBLE WILD PLANTS
A GUIDE TO COLLECTING AND COOKING

Introduction 1
Edible Wild Plants—Description and Photographs 4
Plant Parts—Drawings 63
Glossary 65
Food Types 68
Nutrition Information 70
The Recipes 71
Recipe List According to Types 121
Complete Index 125

EDIBLE WILD PLANTS
A GUIDE TO COLLECTING AND COOKING

by

Ellen Elliott Weatherbee and James Garnett Bruce

Why is there such a great interest in the foraging of wild foods? The beginner is attracted by fresh, free foods which are tasty and nutritious. The casual collector has favorite plants which he harvests avidly, but ignores or does not recognize other wild edibles. The real addict spends a great deal of his spare time either actually collecting plants and processing them, or forever seeking new localities and interchanging ideas and stories with his trusted cronies.

People are attracted to the use of wild plants as part of a "back to nature" interest or with intent to use the knowledge on hiking or backpacking trips. There is a variety of excellent edibles to be found in and around towns, as well as in mature woods and wilderness areas. The greatest number of edibles is found in geographical areas which contain a variety of plant habitats, such as swamps, bogs, streams, stream and river flood plains, fields, various types of woods, roadsides, railroad track embankments, and weedy backyards. The more of these areas available to you throughout the year, the better are your chances of a good supply of wild edibles.

Wild mushrooms are favorites of many people. The fungi come in all shapes, sizes and tastes—several species are even found in winter. For excellent photographs and discussion of mushrooms in this region, see Alex and Helen Smith's *Some Common Mushrooms of Michigan's Parks and Recreation Areas* or the more complete book by Alex Smith entitled *The Mushroom Hunter's Field Guide*.

PRECAUTIONS

The two most obvious points to remember are the importance of correct plant identification and the intelligent use of the environment.

Plants are often difficult to identify when they are young, and great care must be taken to avoid look-alikes which could be bad tasting or even poisonous. There have been many attempts to make easy generalizations about the recognition of unknown plants for their edibility. The wild carrot family, for example, contains many edible species, but also contains the lethal poison hemlock and water hemlock. Be certain to check the plant description and photographs and to pay attention to the proper preparation and time to collect each plant. If possible (and it often is not), find a local authority to help identify them.

It is wise to eat only a small amount of a new food to see if it agrees with you. We have found very few *known* edibles which have bothered any of our students. Day lilies, however, which are lauded as excellent edibles, have produced about 50 cases of upset stomachs over the past few years, and so we have dropped their use.

Some plants are poisonous to touch. Poison ivy and poison sumac are commonly found throughout the region and cause serious itching to sensitive individuals. Even though many adults have never contracted poison ivy or sumac, they often have problems after repeated contact. If you think you have touched the plants, wash as soon as possible with soap and water. Also, nettles, which are an excellent edible, contain stinging hairs along the leaves and stems. Use gloves to collect them to protect your hands.

Be careful not to collect plants from polluted water, in areas where weed killer has been used, or where lead or chemical concentrations are high.

To avoid harming plant populations, the collector should be aware of his impact upon the environment. Be sure to know the types of plants you are collecting. Weedy plants such as nettles and lamb's quarters quickly reproduce and can be collected in abundance. The harvesting of berries, nuts, and fruits does not harm the plant and often helps with dispersal when pits and seeds are thrown away in a new locality. Plants such as wild ginger and ostrich fern could easily be damaged if not collected properly in small quantities. Always leave plenty of the plant to reproduce. To insure that important wildlife foods are not being excessively used, check Martin, Zim and Nelson's *American Wildlife and Plants, A Guide to Wildlife Food Habits*.

It is always necessary to obtain permission to collect plants unless it is on your own property. Many state and county parks will allow collecting, but be sure to obtain permission from their headquarters—be prepared with a list of what you intend to collect and assure them (and stick to it!) of your honesty in collecting only those plants and in quantities in keeping with the plant population. Some park naturalists may show you on maps or in person where good localities are for collecting plants such as blueberries, wild rice, mayapples, and nuts. A telephone call or a quick visit to the owner of a roadside, woods, or field is a necessary courtesy and can result in good feelings for all concerned. Do not be tempted to "snitch." To check ownership of land, look in a county plat book, which is usually available for a nominal fee at the local county building. *Neither the authors nor the publishers accept responsibility for mistakes in identity which may have unfortunate results.*

COLLECTING TECHNIQUES

Collecting techniques can be elaborate or simple depending upon which plants are to be collected. Each collector will find his own list of essential items. The usual array includes a sturdy basket, wax paper, a sharp knife, small trowel, baggies, labels or pieces of paper, pencil, compass, and bug spray. Some plants may require additional collecting equipment. To harvest wild rice, you will need a canoe or kayak and a sheet. A sheet is also helpful to gather mulberries. You will need a shovel to dig ground nuts, leeks and onions, and Jerusalem artichokes. For nettles you need gloves, and for high bush blueberries, cranberries, cat-tails and watercress you need rubber boots or just sneakers and a smile.

PREFACE TO THE SECOND EDITION

This book originally appeared in part as *Edible Wild Plants of the Great Lakes Region*. Two things became apparent as we rapidly went through our first two printings. The book was useful over a much greater area than the title suggested, and the unprinted recipes which we have made for our friends and students over the years were much in demand.

The plants in this book can be found over much of Central and Eastern United States and adjacent Canada. Although wild plants have always been used for food, we have now added years of experimentation with new recipes. We have also adapted existing recipes for both wild and garden plants.

The first part of this book is a field guide, telling "what, where, and how" to collect. The latter part gives the recipes, which are listed alphabetically by the plants which they utilize. We hope you have fun collecting and cooking!

Summer, 1982

E. E. Weatherbee
J. G. Bruce

To order more copies or to share your experiences and recipes, write to us at Box 8253, Ann Arbor, MI 48107.

Figure 1. Asparagus: 1) Fall foliage of asparagus (Ed Rutz); 2) Young shoot, ready to cook; 3) Young shoots, growing along a roadside; 4) Filiform branches; 5) Collection of young shoots, ready to cook.

Asparagus, *Asparagus officinalis*
Lily Family (Liliaceae)

When full grown, this perennial herb has a feathery, Christmas tree-like appearance, often standing over six feet in height. The green branches form most of the photosynthetic areas as the leaves are reduced to scales ½ inch or less long. The small flowers, ¼ inch in size, are greenish white, and the fruits are red berries. In the fall as the plants mature, they turn a conspicuous bright yellow.

However, the plant is harvested in the spring and early summer when the young shoots break through the soil. The young spears do not differ from store-bought asparagus (the plants are the same species) with pointed tips and small triangular scale leaves along the sides.

Locate and note growing areas in the fall as you spot the mature bright yellow plants. In spring and early summer during prime collecting time, you have to be more observant and find the dried stalks left from the previous season bent over or actually lying down. The first shoots appear toward the end of April (early May in northern areas), and the plants continue to produce spears through the end of June. One of our students found some fresh spears in September after a week of rain. Asparagus is found along sunny roadsides, railroad tracks and near garden sites (from which it often "escapes"). Hunting new localities is a favorite pastime for people who enjoy roadside foraging (car botany).

Cut growing shoots 10 to 12 inches tall with a sharp knife at ground level. The plants will produce new shoots every week if there is some rain and warm temperature. Do not return to one plant more than four or five times, or the root stocks will become exhausted and unproductive the following season.

Wild asparagus tastes as good as cultivated asparagus and can be prepared using the same recipes. If the stalks are tough, peel off the outer ⅛ inch of the stalk and use the top portion for a tender vegetable; boil in salted water for eight minutes. The tough lower part of the stalks adds good flavor to soups. Asparagus freezes well after a two minute blanching.

Blueberries, *Vaccinium angustifolium* and *V. corymbosum*
Heath Family (Ericaceae)

Blueberries are perennial shrubs found on sterile acid soils and bogs throughout our area, and are much sought after for their delicious fruit. The size of both the berries and the shrubs varies considerably. The low bush types are usually less than three feet high and are found in dry woods

6 EDIBLE WILD PLANTS

Figure 2. Blueberries: 1) Inspecting blueberry bushes (Ed Rutz); 2) Mature blueberry fruits, ready to eat; 3) Branch of mature clusters; 4) Collected pails of blueberries.

and openings. The most prolific species are found in bogs and acid swamps, where they grow from four to ten feet high. Both types have alternate simple leaves and blue berries which are often borne in clusters. The berry is several seeded and the end opposite the point of attachment bears a characteristic five-lobed remnant of the calyx. There are many plants with blue berries, some of which are poisonous, so be certain that the above characteristics are carefully observed.

The berries ripen from July through the first half of September. Huckleberries, which are closely related, are collected and processed the same as blueberries. Blueberries often grow mixed with poison sumac and sometimes in one to two feet of water, but the berries are well worth collecting. Wear boots and be certain you can identify poison sumac.

To harvest the berries, use a clean metal or plastic pail and pick the berries as clean as possible. A good picker can easily collect one gallon of

EDIBLE WILD PLANTS

berries per hour. Take several small pails, as larger pails, as they fill, become quite heavy and the berries at the bottom tend to be squashed.

The berries require no special processing except for picking them over to remove twigs, leaves, and other debris.

Blueberries are delicious raw as well as cooked in pies, jams, jellies, and syrup. For storage, simply bag and freeze the cleaned berries. Blueberries can also be dried on screening out doors or inside on screens with a gentle source of heat beneath. Store when dry (about 36 hours) in a jar with a lid in a dark place.

Figure 3. Bracken fern: 1) Habitat of bracken fern; 2) A young crozier, 2" high, ready to cook; 3) Mature frond; 4) Young crozier showing three-parted division; 5) Young crozier, 6" high, ready to cook.

Bracken Fern, *Pteridium aquilinum*
Polypody Family (Polypodiaceae)

Bracken fern is the most common fern in our region. It occurs in many types of wooded areas, as well as in meadows, old fields, roadsides and railroad embankments. This fern spreads by underground stems from which leaves arise at scattered intervals. The leaves, or fronds, are triangular in outline and are approximately parallel to the ground. This fern may occur in great abundance in drier sites and cover many acres. The growth may be so dense that sometimes it is impossible to see the ground. In the spring there are numerous dead fronds from the previous season lying on the ground. The young leaves are easily recognized when they come up from the typically three-divided fiddle head. At the point of junction of the three parts are found two black shiny areas, on which ants can be frequently seen. The young fiddle head, which is the curled young leaf, is covered with shiny silver and brown hairs, giving it a silvery green appearance which is often flecked with brown. There is no harm done to the bracken population by collecting a few leaves as the young croziers or fiddleheads are abundant.

Collect the young fronds in early to mid-spring when under ten inches tall. Cook in boiling salted water for about eight minutes. Serve with butter and salt or add to soups or casseroles. Bracken fern is eaten in the Orient, and the young shoots, preserved in a delicious soy mixture, can be purchased in Oriental food stores.

There is a report from Japan, however, which indicates that in feeding experiments with bracken fern cooked in unsalted water, rats often develop stomach cancer. When cooked in salted water, the frequency of cancer was much lower. Because of the report, use discretion in eating bracken. If you decide to eat this fern be sure to cook it in salted water.

To preserve, boil in salted water for two minutes, drain, pat dry, place in plastic bags, label, and freeze.

Cat-tails, *Typha angustifolia* and *T. latifolia*
Cat-tail Family (Typhaceae)

Cat-tails occur throughout our area in marshes or wet open habitats, both in wild areas and in town localities. They form large clones which may cover several acres. Their strap-shaped, blunt tipped leaves spiral several times so that in sunlight they take on patterns of alternating light and dark bands. These round tipped leaves develop from a horizontal rhizome which lies buried several inches in the muck. The flower stalk arises centrally among the leaves and consists of very dense male and

EDIBLE WILD PLANTS 9

Figure 4. Cat-tail: 1) Habitat of cat-tails (Bob Anderson); 2) Young spring shoots (Martha Collins); 3) Underground rhizome and mature fruit, winter condition; 4) Mature male and female spikes with male ready to cook (Bob Anderson); 5) and 6) Mature male and female spikes with male ready to cook; 7) Cooked male spikes.

female inflorescences with the pollen producing male above the seed producing female. The flower stalks and some leaves persist through the winter and provide good clues to the presence of these plants.

During spring when you are collecting the young shoots, there is a potentially confusing plant, iris, which is poisonous. However, in contrast to the round tipped leaves of cat-tails, iris has sharp pointed leaves. Later in the season as the plants mature, iris produces beautiful brightly colored flowers which are quite different from the drab spikes of the cat-tail.

Several parts of this plant can be utilized for food. Throughout the year the rhizomes contain starch covered fibers which can be washed out to make a flour. It is messy and time consuming, but fun to try. Strip off the outer layer or skin and separate the fibers in a bowl of cold water. Dip them up and down to loosen the starch. Discard the fibers. Allow the mixture to sit for an hour and then carefully pour off the water. There remains a sludgy flour at the bottom. Mix the settled starch half and half with regular flour to make bread, muffins, or cake.

The young shoots form in the fall, so throughout the winter these 2"-4" shoots can be eaten raw or boiled. In the early spring these shoots elongate and are good to use until they toughen. Cut the young (3' or less) shoots just above the root and carefully remove the outer leaves to reveal the tender core. The top green leaves will be tough so discard them. For a 2' long stem, you will have about 10" of usable inside. This inner core is quite bland and makes a good basis for a wild salad, as well as a boiled vegetable. Boil the shoots in salted water for five minutes. They are also good used as bamboo shoots or mixed with other vegetables and as a pickle (use a bread and butter pickle recipe).

The young male flower spike is an excellent vegetable as it just emerges from its protective leafy sheath in mid to late spring. Wade into the marsh and cut off this male spike (usually about six inches long), leaving the female part behind (to save a messy cleaning later). Boil the young spikes until tender, about ten minutes. Dip in butter and sprinkle with salt. Eat like an ear of corn leaving the tough slender inner core.

If the male spikes are allowed to mature, the yellow pollen can be collected to use in bread. Hold a bag loosely over the spike and tap the plant gently. Blackbirds, which frequently inhabit cat-tail areas, will at this time be protecting their nests by diving frantically at any invader.

The shoots and the spikes freeze well after a two minute blanching.

Chickweed, Stellaria media
Pink Family (Caryophyllaceae)

Chickweed is a low herbaceous annual or perennial with small, opposite, ovate leaves. The leaves are petioled along the lower part of the stem

EDIBLE WILD PLANTS

Figure 5. Chickweed: 1) Growth habit of chickweed; 2) Leafy stem; 3) Leaf attachment to stem.

and sessile in the upper part. The petioles are frequently pubescent. The flowers are white and usually five parted. Each of the petals is deeply split so that there seems to be ten petals. The plant forms extensive patches of bright green in lawns, weedy areas, and dumps. Do not collect in lawns which have been sprayed with weed killer.

Chickweed can be used any time of year that it looks fresh. We have found it growing abundantly even under snow. Since the leaves grow so

12 *EDIBLE WILD PLANTS*

close to the ground, they are often dirty, so wash them thoroughly in running water or by dunking them up and down in a pail of cool water.

Chickweed has a pleasant, distinct flavor and can be used fresh in salads or prepared as a boiled vegetable. It also freezes well after a two minute blanching.

Figure 6. Cranberries: 1) General aspect of cranberry growth; 2) Leaf and flower; 3) Mature cranberries.

Cranberries, *Vaccinium macrocarpon,* and *V. oxycoccos* Heath Family (Ericaceae)

Cranberries are found throughout our area in open, acid bogs. They are very distinctive as a spreading, low, vining plant. The spindly reddish stem bears tough evergreen leaves smaller than the berry. These alternate leaves are dark green above and whitish below. Cranberries often form dense purplish patches covering large areas of the bog floor. The flowers are pink and the fruit is dark red. The berries occur on one or two inch long peduncles.

The berries are ready to use in the fall after the first hard frost. Some bogs do not produce fruit consistently. The biggest berries are those which grow in full sun, often along the edges of the bog mat, near enough to the edge of the water to provide a cool dunking for the collector who ventures too close. Knee high rubber boots are probably the best foot attire.

Wild cranberries look and taste the same as cultivated ones, although they vary much more in size. To prepare, add water to cover and cook until the berries are soft. Strain through a sieve or food mill and add sugar or honey to taste. A squeeze of lemon juice brings out the flavor. Use this strained juice to make cranberry sherbet, cranberry sauce and jellies and juice. The berries keep well for several weeks in the refrigerator and can be frozen raw for year round use.

Figure 7. Dandelion: 1) Flowering condition of dandelion; 2) Rosette leaf pattern.

Dandelion, *Taraxacum officinale*
Composite Family (Compositae)

This herbaceous, perennial rosette is the best known of our weeds. The leaves are coarsely toothed and exude a milky latex if cut. The flowers are bright yellow and are borne on stalks which elevate them several inches above the rosettes. The shoot originates from a tough tap root. Dandelions are found throughout our area in weedy places, fields, and in lawns. The most prolific growth occurs in open areas, but these plants can occur in woods, where they rarely flower but do produce large leaves. Do not collect in lawns which have been sprayed with weed killer.

Collect dandelions in the early spring before the flowers bloom. Cut

14 EDIBLE WILD PLANTS

the rosette one to two inches below ground level and remove in one piece. Do not separate the leaves from the root section until after cleaning. This avoids washing each leaf separately. To clean, hold onto the root and dunk vigorously up and down in a bucket of water. Clean thoroughly or they may be gritty. Cut off the root as close to the leaves as possible. Discard the root and boil the leaves until tender in a small amount of salted water. If the greens are too bitter, drain the water and boil them briefly in fresh water. Serve with butter and salt or add a little vinegar and a few bacon bits. Very young fresh dandelion greens make a tasty salad. Clean the leaves well and serve with vinegar and oil or any other salad dressing suitable for greens. Dandelions are high in vitamin A. To freeze, blanch in boiling water for two minutes, drain, pat dry, bag, label, and place in freezer.

Figure 8. Elderberries: 1) Flowering condition of elderberries (Ed Rutz); 2) Mature fruit; 3) Flower and leaf arrangement; 4) Lenticels on the bark.

Elderberry, *Sambucus canadensis*
Honeysuckle Family (Caprifoliaceae)

Elderberries are soft-wooded shrubs of ditches, swamps, and their borders. The plants have opposite compound leaves, and their stems possess conspicuous white lenticels. The white flowers and dark-purple fruits are in large, open, and relatively flat-topped clusters. The fruit cluster tends to have a more rounded appearance than the flower cluster. If you cut the stem, the central region is filled with a *white* corky pith. The potentially confusing red-berried elder *(Sambucus pubens)*, a poisonous relative, is easily separated by its conical flower and fruit cluster, its red berries, and its *orange* pith. Both species have poisonous vegetative parts.

The plants are most conspicuous in early summer when they flower. Both the flowers and fruit are edible. Collect the flowers by cutting off the entire flower head with a sharp knife. To make elderberry fritters, separate the flower heads into smaller sections (about 1"-2" across) and dip into a flour, milk, and egg batter. Deep fat fry them and serve with maple syrup or powdered sugar.

The dried flowers make a fragrant tea. Discard the stems and place the flowers on newspaper to dry thoroughly in about 48 hours. Store in a jar with a tight fitting lid. To make tea, add a handful of dried flowers to cold water and bring the water almost to a boil. Steep five minutes and serve with honey or sugar.

The berries ripen in late August and are excellent in pies, jams, and jellies. They are usually too tart to eat raw, although if they are dried first, they taste something like blueberries.

Grapes, *Vitis spp.*
Grape Family (Vitaceae)

Grapes are vining, woody perennials best recognized by their alternate simple leaves and tendrils opposite many of the leaves. The leaves may be highly lobed or conspicuously toothed. The fruits are several-seeded purple berries borne in bunches. The greatest danger is to confuse grapes with either Virginia creeper *(Parthenocissus quinquefolia)* or moonseed *(Menispermum canadense)*. Both of these plants have poisonous fruits which resemble grapes. The Virginia creeper, unlike the grape, has palmately compound leaves and the branches of the fruit cluster are conspicuously red. The moonseed differs from grapes in that it has only a single seed per fruit and this seed is a flat semicircle. The leaves of the moonseed are smooth margined and slightly peltate with the leaf stalk

16   EDIBLE WILD PLANTS

Figure 9. Grapes: 1) Grape leaves; 2) Leaf and tendril attachment to stem; 3) Mature fruit of grape; 4) Moonseed (M) and grape (G) leaves; 5) Moonseed (M) and grape (G) petiole attachment; 6) Moonseed fruit; 7) Mature fruit clusters of moonseed.

attached to the blade of the leaf, not at its margin (as in the grape), but just inside the margin onto the leaf surface. The moonseed has no tendrils.

There are many species of grapes growing abundantly throughout our area. Some species grow in wet areas and some in dry places. Most of the vines are high climbers and can reach 50'-60'.

Two parts of the grape plant are used for food, the leaves and the fruit. Very young leaves (under two inches) can be eaten raw in salads, to which they add a lemony taste. The leaves in late spring and early summer are excellent for use in wrapping a variety of stuffings, such as those made of rice, mushrooms, and nuts. Collect 4"-5" leaves which do not have deep sinuses in them, as the stuffing falls out through these cuts when you wrap them. Tie the leaves in bunches of 15-20 leaves and boil them in a salt brine (½ cup of salt for each two quarts of water) for three minutes, then drain and chill. Place a spoonful of stuffing inside each leaf, fold over and put them on a rack over boiling water and steam for 45 minutes.

The grapes are ready to use in late August and September. Most wild species are too tart to eat raw, but are excellent in pies, jellies, and juice.

To preserve the leaves, boil in salt brine as above, then can or freeze. To preserve the fruit, make pies and freeze, utilize in jelly, or freeze or can sweetened juice. If the grapes are especially tart, they can be mixed with apples.

Ground nuts or Indian potato, *Apios americana*
Bean Family (Leguminosae)

These herbaceous vines have alternate, compound leaves often partly folded along the leaf axis. The plant bears clusters of maroon or chocolate flowers, most of which produce a few flat bean-like pods. As the pods weather, they turn brown and split open. In the winter, leafless vining remnants of the plant with a few open pods in the upper parts are often all that can be seen. Underground, the plants produce a series of tuberous growths along their widely spreading roots. The bead-like appearance of these tubers (1-3 inches in diameter) is diagnostic, and the cut surface of a tuber exudes a milky latex just within its periphery.

The vines are found in swamps in relatively open areas or along their borders, roadside ditches, or marshes. They can be harvested anytime of the year, including winter. Occasionally the tubers lie at the surface of the ground, but usually they must be dug with a shovel. Spot the vines and then dig carefully around them. Once you locate the first tuber, follow along the underground root to the next tuber. The tubers are at their best when freshly dug. Do not use the interconnecting roots, as they are tough.

Prepare them as you would potatoes, sliced and sautéed in butter,

18   *EDIBLE WILD PLANTS*

Figure 10. Ground nuts: 1) Twining vine of ground nuts; 2) Leaflets; 3) Flower cluster; 4) Mature fruit; 5) Edible tubers, ready to cook; 6) Cut tuber, showing milky latex.

boiled or baked. They are especially good served with a mustard sauce or sliced and added to other vegetables. Discard the skins as they tend to be tough. Although the tubers can be eaten without cooking, they are not very palatable when raw.

Various Indian tribes and the early settlers made frequent use of the tubers.

A similar plant, hog peanut *(Amphicarpa bracteata),* also has edible tubers. However, only one tuber appears at the root system, the vine is more delicate, there are only three leaves, and the flowers are pink.

Figure 11. Hazelnuts: 1) General aspect of a hazelnut shrub (Bob Anderson) 2) Leaves; 3) Mature fruit with leaves, ready to process; 4) Mature fruit, ready to process.

Hazelnut, *Corylus americana* and *C. cornuta*
Birch Family (Betulaceae)

There are two species of this medium sized shrub. Both form many basal branches and bear alternate coarsely toothed leaves which are somewhat elongate and heart-shaped. The nuts, which develop in late summer, are encased in a distinctive husk which appears as a vase with a ruffled lip. In the beaked hazelnut, this lip is long and protruded, while in the common hazelnut, it is less prominent. The plants occur along borders of wet areas.

The quality and quantity of these nuts varies from shrub to shrub and year to year. In some years, there are especially heavy fruitings (mast years). Hazelnuts are easy to open, as the husk is fairly soft and can be cut or pulled off with a pair of pliers or a nut cracker. Some people are allergic to the fuzziness of the nut and need to wear gloves when collecting them.

The nuts can be eaten raw, or cooked whole or in pieces in cakes and cookies. Hazelnuts can be chopped finely with a knife or blender and sprinkled on baked goods or vegetables.

Squirrels and chipmunks make extensive use of hazelnuts, so collect conservatively with the needs of wildlife in mind. Often it is difficult to find very many nuts in early September when they are ripe, as the animals can be quite complete in their gathering. After extracting the nut meats, keep them in a refrigerator or freezer to prevent spoilage.

Hickory nuts, *Carya spp.*
Walnut Family (Juglandaceae)

Hickory trees are major components of our drier forests. They also frequently occur along roadsides. The plants have alternate, compound leaves, and the leaflets are ovate to obovate. Two of our most common types, both of which have edible nuts, are the shagbark and the false shagbark hickory. These trees have scaly peeling bark, making them easy to recognize. The smooth bark hickories also have edible nuts, although some have a medicinal taste.

The nuts are ready to harvest when they fall to the ground in early fall. The outer husks of the nuts are easy to remove, but the nutshell is extremely hard and may require a vise for easy cracking. The nut is placed in the vise with its axis oriented vertically or horizontally, with the jaws of the vise compressing it as shown in the figures. Once cracked, the shell is further opened using a pair of good grade wire clippers. You can easily produce a pint an hour in this fashion.

EDIBLE WILD PLANTS 21

Figure 12. Hickory: 1) Mature hickory tree; 2) Leaves with ripening nut; 3) Bark of shagbark hickory; 4) Nut with protective husk; 5) Method of cracking hickory nut; 6 and 7) Nuts in vise; 8) Extracting nut meats with wire cutters; 9) Collection of nuts ready to eat and broken nuts and wire cutters used to extract the nut meats.

Figure 13. High bush cranberry: 1) General aspect of a high bush cranberry; 2) Mature fruit, ready to process; 3) Mature fruit with leaves.

High bush cranberry, *Viburnum trilobum*
Honeysuckle Family (Caprifoliaceae)

High bush cranberries are shrubs found in low, wet areas and are easily recognized when in fruit by their drooping clusters of bright red berries which have flat white seeds. These plants have paired three-lobed, maple-shaped leaves and multiple stems which usually do not exceed ten feet in height. The branching is opposite, and in the winter when the berries are ripe, there are conspicuous large smooth buds.

The European high bush cranberry *(V. opulus)* closely resembles the high bush cranberry. It is frequently planted ornamentally, but is unfortunately inedible because of its persistent bitter taste. There is no reliable, easy method of discerning the two types, except to try small amounts from moist, wild looking areas. The cultivated species will never attain proper sweetness.

The wild berries are collected any time after the first hard frost. They have a bitter, medicinal taste when raw. To prepare them, cover the fruit with cold water and bring to a gentle boil. A slice of orange peel cuts the bad odor. Simmer for 15 minutes or until the berries are soft. Put the juice and the berries through a sieve or a food mill. Add sugar or honey to taste. After cooking and then cooling, these berries resemble regular cranberries in taste and can be used for sherbet, sauce, jelly, and juice. The sieved mixture can be frozen in plastic freezer cartons.

Figure 14. Japanese knotweed: 1) Knotweed locality (Ellen Weatherbee); 2) Winter condition; 3) Leaf; 4) Leaf attachment to stem; 5) Young shoots, ready to cook, 5" high; 6) Young shoot, ready to cook, with leaves, 6" high.

Japanese knotweed, or Mexican bamboo, *Polygonum cuspidatum*
Smartweed Family (Polygonaceae)

This is a perennial herb which grows to six or seven feet in height. The young shoots resemble asparagus when they emerge from the ground with their large, thick succulent shoots. The older stalks have a reddish color and the leaves are simple, heart-shaped, and alternate. Associated with every leaf is a small sleeve of plant tissue which actually encircles the stem for a short distance above the point of attachment of the leaf. In the spring, the old growth from the previous year is frequently still standing and resembles a small forest of stiff, upright rattles. These old shoots have a hollow, empty clothes-hanger-in-the-closet sound when you brush into them. The plant is a weedy escape and is found around old home sites and in disturbed areas.

The time to collect Japanese knotweed is early spring just as the spring wildflowers are at their peak. The harvesting season for each locality is only two to three weeks, during which time the young shoots are tender. Cut the young growth under ten inches tall with a sharp knife. Take as many as desired, as the plant quickly produces new shoots. Return in three to five days when another batch will be ready. If the locality is extensive, the whole year's supply can be gathered at one time.

Japanese knotweed makes a good pie which tastes similar to rhubarb, a good sauce (stewed with the addition of sugar or honey) or a good vegetable when cooked 10 minutes in a small amount of boiling, salted water. It can be frozen by blanching for two minutes, patting dry before placing in freezer bags, labeling and freezing.

Jerusalem artichoke, *Helianthus tuberosus*
Composite Family (Compositae)

The Jerusalem artichoke is a species of sunflower and is a tall perennial herb. The stem has opposite leaves basally which become alternate in the upper parts of the stem. The leaves are simple and coarsely toothed. There are usually three prominent veins (the midvein and two laterals) extending into the blade from the base of the leaf. The leaves and stems are covered by stiff hairs which make it difficult to freely slide your hand along them. The yellow-orange flowers blossom in September and are small sunflowers, being only two to three inches across. There are a number of species of sunflowers, but this is the only one with large conspicuous tubers. Examination of the tubers shows opposite buds along the swollen segments. Until you learn to recognize this plant you will find

EDIBLE WILD PLANTS

Figure 15. Jerusalem artichokes: 1) Mature late summer Jerusalem artichoke plants (Ed Rutz); 2) Flowering condition; 3) Three-veined leaf pattern; 4) Hairy opposite leaves and stem; 5) Mature tuber, showing bud pairing; 6) Collection of tubers, ready to eat; 7) Digging for tubers in late fall (Ellen Weatherbee).

yourself examining numerous related species which lack the tubers. Jerusalem artichokes often form dense stands along roadsides and in garden sites. They reproduce quickly, as the tubers are viable even when cut into small pieces. The plants are easiest to spot in mid to late summer when they may reach ten to twelve feet.

Collect the tubers in the fall, winter, or early spring before the vegetative growth begins. Once the young shoots have begun to grow in the spring, the tubers become mushy and insipid.

The tubers range in size from that of a thick pencil to a large chunky carrot. Dig around the base of the plants with a shovel. The tubers spread out and down from the stalk. In dense stands, the larger tubers often occur on the periphery of the patch. The tubers clean easily by dunking them up and down in a bucket of water or by scrubbing hard with a vegetable brush.

The tubers are crisp and tasty and can be eaten raw in salads or served with appetizer dips. Rub the cut slices with lemon juice to prevent discoloration. For a boiled vegetable, cook the tubers about eight minutes in boiling salted water. Serve hot with melted butter or a mustard sauce. The skins tend to be a bit tough and can be removed prior to cooking.

The tubers will keep for several weeks in the refrigerator. It is best, however, to collect them as needed. Freshly dug tubers are very low in calories.

Lamb's quarters, *Chenopodium album*
Goosefoot Family (Chenopodiaceae)

This herbaceous annual has foliage of bluish-green color. This distinctive coloration is due to small white granules which occur all over the plant, but are most concentrated near the growing tip. Leaves are alternate and simple with irregularly lobed margins. Under ideal conditions, mature plants may grow more than six feet in height, although two to four feet is the average size.

Lamb's quarters grow in sunny localities as a common weed in gardens, lawns and construction sites from mid-April through September. Collect young growth, preferably under four inches tall or the top several inches of larger plants. Maturing plants soon become too tough to use. Growth is profuse and growing plants are often of the same size, so they can be easily cut "en masse" with a knife or scissors. Check carefully to remove all unwanted plants before use.

Lamb's quarters is related to spinach and can substitute as the spinach in recipes. After gathering, rinse thoroughly, boil in salted water until just tender, about seven minutes, and serve with salt and butter. This

EDIBLE WILD PLANTS

Figure 16. Lamb's quarters: 1) General growth pattern of lamb's quarters; 2) Young plant; 3) Tender young leaves, ready to cook.

species is one of the tastiest of our wild plants; the greens are good in soups and casseroles. To preserve, drop into boiling salted water for two minutes, drain, pat dry, package in plastic bags, label and freeze. The greens are nutritionally high in calcium, vitamin A and vitamin C.

28	EDIBLE WILD PLANTS

Figure 17. Maples: 1), 2), and 3) Various types of maple leaves; 4) Typical winged fruit (key); 5) Terminal buds on a twig; 6) Opposite branching pattern; 7) Sap dripping from tree in late winter.

Maple, *Acer spp.*
Maple Family (Aceraceae)

Maple trees are common throughout our area in woods and swamps. Most abundant are the red and sugar maples and the box elder. All maples have opposite leaves, most of which are simple and palmately veined. The leaves of the box elder are compound. Maples can be recognized in the winter by their opposite bud pairs. The main difficulty with winter identification is confusion with the ashes which also have opposite leaves. The buds and twigs of the ashes are, however, thicker and stubbier than that of maples. Again, the box elder is exceptional. However, the distinctive waxy bloom on the twigs of the box elder does not occur on the ashes.

All species of maples can be used to make maple products. Tap the trees in late winter when the nights remain cold and the daytime temperatures warm into the 40's and 50's. To tap a tree, drill a two inch long hole through the bark about three feet above the ground. Insert a hollow twig, a small hollow metal pipe, or a commercial maple spile (available from good hardware stores). A tree one foot in diameter can support two spiles while larger trees can handle three or four. Sugaring season is from about mid-February to mid-March, although we have collected sap as early as mid-January during a warm spell. Once the buds begin to enlarge in March, the sap darkens and tastes "buddy." Fresh sap can be drunk plain, used as a base for teas, or used as the liquid for cooking vegetables.

To make syrup, the clear sap must be reduced considerably in volume which requires rapid boiling. This usually is done out-of-doors because of the amount of water which must be boiled off. A wood fire is traditional for "sugaring," although many people now have homemade setups using propane gas burners. The syrupy sap burns easily when it begins to thicken and turn golden brown, and it is best at that time to bring it indoors to regulate the heat with your stove. Insert a thermometer and watch carefully. Cook gently to 219°F. If maple sugar is desired, continue cooking carefully to 234°F when the sap will have thickened considerably and can be poured into maple sugar molds or muffin tins.

If you keep the syrup longer than two weeks, sterilize it in a boiling water bath to prevent spoilage.

May apple, *Podophyllum peltatum*
Barberry Family (Berberidaceae)

May apples are perennial herbs which bloom in May and often form large colonies. The flowers, and later the fruit, are borne in the crotch of a fork (a pair) of leaves. The leaves are umbrella-like (peltate) being

30 EDIBLE WILD PLANTS

Figure 18. May apple: 1) May apple plant in spring; 2) Leaves; 3) Mature fruit, ready to eat; 4) Flower in spring; 5) Mature fruit, ready to eat.

attached in their center. The whole plant is about two feet in height. The fruit is the size of a small egg and has a very pleasant tropical fruit smell when it ripens. The vegetative parts of the plant and the unripe fruit are poisonous, so do not eat the fruit until it has lost its green color and has ripened by turning yellow and acquiring the fruity odor. Place slightly green fruit indoors on newspaper, and it will ripen in a few days.

May apples are found in open rich woods and along wooded roadsides. They will tolerate some sunlight. Since the plants are easy to spot in the spring, remember the localities, because when the fruit is ready in mid-August, the plants are often brown and lying on the ground.

To prepare May apples, cut off the stem and blossom ends and cut the fruit into quarters; cover with cold water in a pan and bring to a gentle boil. Simmer the mixture until the fruit is tender, then put through a sieve or food mill. The mixture can be frozen at this point. May apples make a delicious chiffon pie and a good juice and jelly. Small amounts of juice add flavor to other fruit juices, such as orange, lemon, and apricot.

Milkweed, *Asclepias syriaca*
Milkweed Family (Asclepiadaceae)

The common milkweed, a familiar plant of fields and roadsides, is a little-branched perennial herb, and is one of the best tasting wild plants. Its opposite simple leaves are elliptical in outline and pale green. Milky sap exudes when the plant is cut. The flowers are pink and clustered in umbels. Although there may be 50 or more flowers to a cluster, only a few fruits will develop. The pale green fruit is swollen basally, tapers to a tip, with a rough textured surface.

In the spring when the young shoots are collected, the plant emerges from the ground with its velvety hairy leaves folded upward along the short, unbranched stem. At this time of year it is easy to confuse milkweed with dogbane *(Apocynum androsaemifolium)* which is bitter and unpalatable. Both milkweed and dogbane have milky sap, opposite simple leaves, and look similar, especially in the spring. The presence of the previous season's stalks with a few old fruits is good evidence for identifying the young shoots. Check the following characteristics to differentiate the two plants:

	Milkweed	*Dogbane*
1) Leaf surface	velvety hairy	smooth
2) Leaf edge	prominent marginal vein	no obvious marginal vein
3) Mature plant growth form	essentially unbranched	much branched
4) Flower cluster	umbel	cyme
5) Fruit shape	swollen base, tapered tip	long, thin, pencil-like

32   EDIBLE WILD PLANTS

Figure 19. Milkweed: 1) Growth habit of milkweed (2½ feet tall); 2) Flower buds (top) and flowers (bottom); 3) Leaf, showing venation and milky juice; 4) Young pods.

The young milkweed shoots can be found from mid-April until mid-June. Cut the shoots when they are 8" tall or less. Collect the buds when they first form in late May or June. These tight clusters of buds are excellent. Collect the young pods in June or July while they are still firm and under two inches long. Cut both ends of the pods just before cooking to insure freshness. All parts must be specially processed due to a bitter component in all parts of the plant. Bring a large kettle of water to a rapid boil and add cleaned milkweed parts. Return to a boil and boil hard one minute. Drain and discard the water. Repeat twice. Serve with butter and salt. Milkweed is good served in a cream or cheese sauce.

Milkweed also freezes well after being processed in the three waters, then drained, patted dry, bagged in plastic bags and frozen. Milkweed pods make good pickles, using either a dill pickle recipe or a bread and butter pickle recipe.

Mints, *Mentha spp.,* Catnip, *Nepeta cataria,*
Beebalm, Bergamot, Wild oregano, *Monarda spp.*
Mint Family (Labiatae)

Mints are herbs with square stems, opposite simple leaves, and an aromatic odor. There are other plants which are not mints which have square stems and opposite leaves, but these plants lack the aromatic odor. The leaves vary considerably from species to species. Some mint variations are:
1. placement of leaves (either having a short stalk or lying closely against the main stem).
2. adaptability to winter conditions (some retain a viable root system and numerous leaves, while others die back to a few tiny green shoots, if any).
3. habitat (most of our native mints live in wet areas such as moist meadows, swamps, and edges of streams; however, both catnip and beebalm prefer sandy, well drained sites).
4. smell (some species have subtle, almost earthy smells while others have a sharp, brilliant refreshing smell; some smell like peppermint candy and others smell like spearmint).

Collect mints any time they are fresh-looking and green. The major use is as a tea plant and for that they are excellent both fresh or dried. To use fresh, wash a handful of stems and leaves thoroughly, cut into 1″ pieces and place in cold water to cover. Bring almost to a boil and let steep for ten minutes. Add more water if too strong. Serve hot or cold with honey or sugar.

Mint leaves are high in vitamin C and vitamin A.

Mint jelly is excellent made from any of the wild mints. Use the recipe found in boxes of commercial pectin.

Dry mint leaves on newspaper until crinkly dry to preserve for future use. Store in air tight jars in a dry, dark place.

Figure 20. Mints: 1) Mint stem; 2) Cross-section of mint stem; 3) Leaf attachment; 4) Leaf attachment; 5) Flowers of beebalm; 6) General growth pattern.

Figure 21. Mulberries: 1) Mulberry tree; 2) Leaves; 3) Leaves and mature fruit, ready to eat.

White mulberry, *Morus alba*
Mulberry Family (Moraceae)

The white mulberry is a small tree found in disturbed sites such as old fields, waste land in towns, and among home plantings. Its leaves are frequently shaped like mittens, and young plants usually have leaves that are lobed. The leaves are toothed and alternate. Bark of young trees and younger growth on older trees is tan. The fruits resemble blackberries in shape and have a small stalk at one end. The color of the white mulberry fruits varies from white to red or dark-purple.

There is also a native mulberry, the infrequently encountered red mulberry *(Morus rubra)* which occurs in flood plains and dune forests. Although less common than the white mulberry, its fruits are large and sweet.

Mulberry trees are either male or female with the fruit being formed only on the female tree. Collect the ripe fruits by hand picking or by placing a sheet underneath the tree and shaking it (a quick method, but the collection will contain twigs and green berries also).

The raw fruit has a bland taste, but is good made into jams, jelly, or pies. The green stem on the berries can be left on, since these stems are tasteless and tedious to remove.

To freeze, cover clean mulberries with sugar or a sugar syrup. Mulberry jam and frozen pies keep almost indefinitely.

Nettles, *Urtica dioica*
Nettle Family (Urticaceae)

Nettles are opposite leaved perennials of swamps, floodplains, and other wet areas. The leaves are regularly and coarsely toothed. The flowers are wind pollinated and conspicuous only for numbers, as they are not showy. The whole plant is covered with stiff white hairs which are fairly scattered. These are the urticating hairs and can cause a dermatitis when they inject irritating compounds into the skin. The stem is ribbed. The leaves may have a purplish cast in the winter, but during the growing season the whole plant is dark green. Mature plants can reach five to six feet and often form dense growths covering much of a swamp understory.

Nettles should be collected with rubber gloves so that the plant will not touch the skin. The stinging feels like a mosquito bite, but is prolonged and often more severe. The joy of collecting nettles is that the greens taste very good, are high in vitamin C and vitamin A and can be collected abundantly with little fear of damaging the plant as cutting stimulates growth.

The greens are best in early to mid-spring and again in the fall, when there is frequently another surge of growth. To collect, cut off the top several inches of the plant with a knife or a pair of scissors. Once the plants are over six inches tall, they are too stringy and tough to use. If you must collect them when the plants are tall, use only the top pair of leaves.

EDIBLE WILD PLANTS

Figure 22. Nettles: 1) Summer condition of mature nettles; 2) Leaf attachment and stem; 3) Young shoots, 4" high, ready to process.

As soon as the nettles are boiled for a minute, they lose their ability to sting, although they need to be cooked eight to ten minutes to become tender. Serve with butter and salt. They also mix well with other vegetables and make a fine addition to soups and casseroles.

Nettles are easily frozen following blanching of cleaned young shoots in boiling water for two minutes. The leaves can also be dried in one layer on newspaper and stored tightly covered in a dark place.

New Jersey tea, *Ceanothus americanus*
Buckthorn Family (Rhamnaceae)

This low woody shrub is a distinctive member of drier woods and open areas. In woods it tends to have an open growth form and in sunny,

38   *EDIBLE WILD PLANTS*

Figure 23. New Jersey tea: 1) Open growth form of New Jersey tea; 2) Close-up of overwintering discs which supported the fruit; 3) Three-veined leaf pattern with flowers.

open areas, it has a more common and characteristic bunched shrubbiness. The leaves have three principal veins, one mid vein and two strong laterals which emerge from the point of attachment of the leaf stalk. Clustered white flowers surmount stalks which extend above the leaves. After the little fruits fall off, the small white discs which supported the fruits remain attached to the plant. As numerous fruits develop from a single flower cluster, there are many of these "saucers" which are very conspicuous. They may persist for several years and are a distinctive identifying feature.

New Jersey tea makes an excellent beverage and is well worth finding. It was used during the Revolutionary War when Oriental tea was difficult to obtain.

Collect the leaves any time they are green from mid-spring to mid-fall, although when the shrub is in flower is the best time. Dry the leaves in one layer on newspaper until crinkly dry. Store them in lidded jars.

To make tea, place a handful of crushed leaves in a quart of cold water. Bring almost to a boil and steep for ten minutes. Serve with honey or sugar.

Figure 24. Onions: 1) Wild leeks in spring (10" tall); 2) Bulb and fruit in summer (12" tall) of leeks; 3) Bulb and fruit in winter (12" tall) of leeks 4) Mature black seeds of leeks; 5) Wild onions in summer (11" tall); 6) Wild onions with bulb and leaves.

Onions, *Allium spp.*
Lily Family (Liliaceae)

Onions are bulb-bearing herbaceous plants found in woods, flood plains, swamps, and fields. In early summer, there are small flowers which are in a single umbel on top of the green stem. Positive identification of wild onions is given by their distinctive odor. Different species of wild onions are found in a variety of habitats. Wild leeks occur in rich deciduous woods both in upland dry areas and low areas. Wild leeks are delicious; in West Virginia they are called "wild ramps" and each year there is a festival in the spring to celebrate the new crop. Although wild leeks can be used year around, they are at their peak about two weeks after the leaves appear. Dig the leeks gently with a shovel or trowel, being careful to leave plenty to reproduce. Use both the leaves and the white bulbs. Wild chives and wild garlic are very tasty in the spring and early summer, although the bulbs can be collected year around. The leaves of all species tend to be milder than the bulbs.

Wild onions are used fresh, either raw or cooked. They are often quite strong-flavored. If a milder flavor is desired, boil the onions for a few minutes and discard the water. Repeat. Sautéed onions are delicious, as are soups made with chopped onions. Wild onions freeze well and are useful for adding flavor to soups and casseroles.

To freeze, clean the onions well with a vegetable brush, chop coarsely and boil for two minutes. Drain, pat dry with toweling, label, and freeze.

Ostrich Fern, *Matteuccia struthiopteris*
Polypody Family (Polypodiaceae)

Ostrich fern is a large fern with two types of leaves. The long graceful green fronds (up to four or five feet) form a rosette in whose center are the shorter, stiffly erect reproductive fronds. These reproductive fronds are green only during their early development; the rest of the year, through the following spring, these persistent fronds are dark brown. In the spring during collecting season, the young green fiddleheads are covered by numerous small brown, rather flaky scales. Both types of fronds possess a conspicuous groove along their leaf stalks. The presence of this groove combined with the rosette growth form and the two types of fronds makes for a positive identification of ostrich fern. The plants are found in wet areas, especially in flood plains.

There are two other ferns in our area which are potentially confusing with the ostrich fern, although both lack the characteristic groove in the

Figure 25. Ostrich fern: 1) A mature clump of ostrich fern, 2' high; 2) Fertile fronds, 10" high; 3) Groove in fertile frond; 4) Young crozier showing groove, 4" high, ready to cook; 5) Collection of young croziers, ready to cook.

leaf stalk. One, the cinnamon fern *(Osmunda cinnamomea)* is a rosette with centrally placed reproductive fronds. In contrast to the ostrich fern, however, cinnamon fern fiddleheads are fuzzy, not scaly, and the reproductive fronds are not stiffly persistent, as they die down in the spring of the year in which they are produced. The other look alike, sensitive fern *(Onoclea sensibilis),* has stiffly erect and peristent reproductive fronds.

However, this is not a rosette fern and it lacks the groove seen in the ostrich fern leaf stalk.

Ostrich fern is a delicious wild treat which is a joy to find and to eat. It is quite abundant in the northern part of our area, and is "locally abundant" in the southern portion. The fiddleheads (the young curled-up shoots) are occasionally sold in gourmet food stores at exorbitant prices. Maine and Nova Scotia are areas of intense collecting.

Since the fern is not common in some areas, take care not to over collect. Gather the young leaves when they are 5" to 8" tall; cut only one or two leaves per plant, using a sharp knife to avoid tugging up the roots. New fiddleheads will continue to come up every few days, so one locality can be harvested several times over its two week growing season. The time each area is ready will vary from the end of April through the third week of May.

After collecting the shoots, wash them well and remove the brown scales where the fiddlehead is rolled. Recut the base of the stalk just before plunging into boiling, salted water. Boil until just tender, about ten minutes. The fiddleheads are delicious served with butter and a dab of vinegar, or they can be served with a cheese of Hollandaise sauce or cooked in a marinade and then chilled.

To freeze, drop the clean, recut shoots into boiling, salted water. Boil two minutes, drain, pat dry, label, and freeze.

Pawpaw, *Asimina triloba*
Custard-apple Family (Annonaceae)

These small native trees have large dark-green, pointed leaves which smell like motor oil when bruised. They turn yellow when the fruit is ripe. The buds have folded fuzzy brown bud scales. The tree bark is dark, and relatively smooth except for the many small whitish bumps or lenticels distributed over its surface. The wood is weak, so even when animals climb trees to collect the fruit, the tops are easily broken. The ripe fruit can usually be shaken out for gathering. The fruit is the most distinctive part of this plant and resembles a stubby banana. The green skin turns black as the fruit ripens. The pulp is orange and custardy with a pleasant taste and fragrance reminding one of a tropical fruit. In the pulp are the large, smooth, brown seeds.

In Michigan, pawpaw trees are not found north of the middle of the lower peninsula. They often form extensive clones (clusters) and are restricted to low lying areas, usually flood plains, although they also grow

EDIBLE WILD PLANTS

Figure 26. Pawpaws: 1) General habitat of pawpaws (Bob Anderson; 2) Picking pawpaws (Jim Bruce); 3) Bark with lenticels; 4) Leaves; 5) Collection of pawpaws, ready to eat.

along the borders of swamps. In the fall, collect fully ripe, slightly soft fruit after the first frost. Handle gently as they bruise easily.

To prepare the pulp, remove the seeds, either by hand or by putting the pulp through a sieve or food mill. Pawpaws make good pies, jelly and ice cream.

44   EDIBLE WILD PLANTS

Figure 27. Pokeweed: 1) General habit of pokeweed (Juno Bruce); 2) Flowering condition; 3) Young plant with leaves, 6" high, ready to prepare; 4) Stem cut open to show diaphragms; 5) Mature plant with fruit.

Pokeweed, *Phytolacca americana*
Pokeweed Family (Phytolaccaceae)

This perennial herb is a large, unpleasant smelling plant often reaching eight feet in height. The older stems are purple with conspicuous internal diaphragms. The leaves are large, simple, and alternate. The plants are derived from a large underground root stock which may be tremendous in size. The flowers are white and are borne in racemes, which are opposite to leaves. The fruits, when ripe, are deep purple. The young shoots as they first come up may be difficult to recognize. They are green with a hint of yellow. There are usually some of the previous year's stalks lying around in the same area. Some of the best localities are under black locust stands, although they are also found in disturbed areas of other woods, along roadsides and in old fields.

The root is poisonous, and the berries and older shoots may also contain some of the poison. The young shoots are ready to collect from early May to the latter part of June. Often new seedlings appear in August and September.

Cut the young shoots when they are no more than eight inches tall. There is no need to leave any shoots as more will grow easily in five to seven days. It is almost impossible to harm a poke plant. Wash the leaves well and place them in rapidly boiling, salted water. Repeat twice more. Continue boiling eight to ten minutes in the third water. This repeated boiling extracts any poison which may have spread into the young shoots. Pokeweed mixes well with sauces and in soups, but is especially good as served boiled in the southern U.S. as "poke sallet"—with lots of butter, vinegar, and bacon bits. The leaves are low in calories and high in vitamin A and vitamin C.

To freeze, process as above for the boiled greens, cool, pat dry, label, and freeze.

Purslane, *Portulaca oleracea*
Purslane Family (Portulacaceae)

Purslane is a prostrate spreading annual with thick, fleshy, alternate leaves shaped like little paddles. The stems are reddish and the seeds, which are almost always present on some part of the plant, are small and black little open vase like pods. The leaves are often grouped into flattened clusters. The plant is a frequent garden weed, sometimes assuming dominance when the garden is unweeded. In more shaded parts of the garden, the plant is less prostrate and may rise a foot or more. Purslane also grows in window boxes and along city side walks. Its season extends from early summer through the fall.

Cut the stems with a sharp knife. If more shoots are desired, leave the root in the ground and more stems will grow within a week.

The taste of cooked purslane is good, and the plants do not cook down very much. The shoots can also be eaten raw in salads or mixed with cheese or sour cream dips.

To prepare, wash the stems well and place in boiling, salted water for five minutes. Drain and serve with butter. The stems mix very well in casseroles and soups, and make good pickles (use a dill or a bread and butter pickle recipe). Purslane is low in calories and contains some vitamin A and vitamin C.

To freeze, boil the shoots two minutes, drain, pat dry, label and freeze.

Figure 28. Purslane: 1) Growth pattern of purslane, ready to eat; 2) Leaves; 3) Leaves and stem with flower buds.

Raspberries, Blackberries, and Thimbleberries, *Rubus spp.*
Rose Family (Rosaceae)

These are woody perennial plants. Some species form dense brush stands and some trail low to the ground. They occur in waste open ground and along edges of thickets and woods. The plants have alternate leaves which are compound or palmately lobed. The plants are usually armed with spines although some species lack these altogether. Thimbleberries are found in the more northern regions. When raspberries and thimbleberries are removed from the parent plant, the central peduncle of the fruit is left on the plant. This results in the thimble-like fruit which has a hollow center. Blackberries, however, retain the central receptacle so that the fruit lacks a hollow center when picked. Wild berries can be

EDIBLE WILD PLANTS 47

Figure 29. Raspberries and blackberries: 1) Growth pattern of raspberries; 2) Leaves and fruit; 3) Mature and unripe fruit; 4) Blackberry stem; 5) Black raspberry stem; 6) Red raspberry stem.

found in great abundance in July and August, depending upon the species, the weather conditions, and the location. Although some are sweeter than others, almost all are excellent raw and are also good in pies, juices, jams, and jellies. To freeze, cover the berries with a sugar syrup or with granulated sugar.

A flavorful tea can be made from the leaves of any of the species. Use the leaves either fresh or completely dried. Combine a small handful of leaves with one quart of cold water. Bring to just under a boil and steep eight to ten minutes. Serve with honey or sugar, if desired.

To dry the leaves, collect the green leaves on a dry day, preferably when the plant is in flower. Spread them in a single layer on newspaper indoors or use a plant dryer turned to very low heat. The leaves are ready for storage when they are crinkly dry. Store in airtight jars in a dark place.

Sassafras, *Sassafras albidum*
Laurel Family (Lauraceae)

Sassafras is one of the best known of the edible wild plants. It is a clone forming tree which can achieve considerable size. The leaves are distinctive because of their various mitten-like shapes. The twigs of young growth are green while the bark of older stems and of the central trunk is salmon pink, which is especially noticeable when the bark is scraped. The best distinguishing feature is the aromatic odor which is found in all parts of the plant and is especially prominent in the roots. The branching pattern of the trees consists of a central trunk from which lateral branches spread almost at right angles and then turn up near their ends. These turned up ends produce a candelabra pattern, which is particularly helpful for spotting these trees in the winter.

The roots may be collected any time for tea, although the tea has been traditionally used as a spring tonic. Pull or dig the roots of a sassafras sapling which is about 2" in diameter and 6' to 10' tall; larger specimens are usually too difficult to handle. Since there is a network of roots between trees, the roots may be dug without permanently damaging the plants. Some people prefer to make a major once-a-year digging and process one large root from a big tree. Tea is also made from the bark and leaves, but the flavor is inferior. Use the roots fresh or dried on newspaper or racks for 48 hours or until dry.

To prepare the roots for tea, scrub them thoroughly with a vegetable brush and cold water. Cut them into 3" to 4" segments and place in a pan. Cover with cold water and bring to just under a boil. Steep for ten minutes or until a dusky pink. Serve with honey. The leaves are good dried and used as an addition to soups for flavoring and a slight thickening.

There is evidence that sassafras roots can cause cancer, so check the current FDA advice.

EDIBLE WILD PLANTS 49

Figure 30. Sassafras: 1) Clone of young sassafras trees; 2) A root ready for stripping (Jim and Roch Anderson); 3) Dried root bark, ready to brew; 4) Leaves.

Figure 31. Sheep sorrel: 1) Growth pattern of sheep sorrel, ready to cook; 2) Leaves and stem.

Sheep sorrel, *Rumex acetosella*
Smartweed Family (Polygonaceae)

Sheep sorrel is an herbaceous weed with tufted basal leaves and scattered leaves along the upright flower stalk. The leaves are arrow-head shaped. The reddish flower and fruiting stalks are quite conspicuous when many of these little plants grow together in fields. They also grow in waste areas, lawns, and wood's borders. The individual flowers are less than ¼" and the whole plant rarely exceeds ten inches in height.

Sheep sorrel is best in the spring and early summer when there is new growth, but it can be used any time. Since it is a weed, there are no cautions on collecting. Sheep sorrel has a pleasant, refreshing, tangy lemon taste both raw and cooked. Children especially like sheep sorrel leaves raw.

The raw leaves are good plain or chopped up in salads. The cooked leaves are excellent in soups and go particularly well with a chicken base. The leaves can be eaten as a boiled vegetable, but they will cook down considerably.

To preserve, boil the leaves for one minute, drain, pat dry, label, and freeze.

EDIBLE WILD PLANTS

Figure 32. Spice bush: 1) General aspect of spice bush (Ed Rutz); 2) Winter condition; 3) Lenticels of the bark; 4) Fruit and leaf attachment; 5) Leaves; 6) Buds.

Spicebush, *Lindera benzoin*
Laurel Family (Lauraceae)

This much branched shrub is a native of rich, moist sites such as swamps and flood plains. It has alternate simple unlobed leaves. The bark is relatively smooth, dark gray, and spotted with small white lenticels. The flowers and buds are borne clustered near the ends of the numerous short twigs. The buds are often nearly spherical in shape. The flowers are yellow and appear before the leaves in the spring. The fruit is berry-like

52   *EDIBLE WILD PLANTS*

and red. The most distinctive feature is, however, the odor which is spicy, pungent, and almost medicinal. Cutting several branches from several shrubs does not permanently harm the plants.

Early settlers used the berries as a substitute for allspice, but the best use is for a refreshing tea. Cut the twigs with pruning shears or a sharp knife. When ready to make tea, cut the twigs into 2" or 3" inch sections and add to cold water. Bring almost to a boil and let steep for ten minutes. The tea tastes good at this point, but will be almost colorless unless steeped for another 20 minutes. Depending on the strength of the twigs, it takes about a handful of cut twigs per quart of water.

The twigs may be frozen, but since they are available all year around at approximately the same strength, there is little need for preservation.

Figure 33. Strawberries: 1) Strawberry plant in flower; 2) Mature fruit, ready to eat (Julie Weatherbee); 3) Leaves and mature fruit; 4) Leaves.

Strawberries, *Fragaria virginiana*
Rose Family (Rosaceae)

Strawberries are rosette perennial herbs with numerous three-divided compound leaves. Each leaflet is coarsely toothed. The plant also produces runners which are stems which spread away from the parent plant to start new plants. The plant has white five-parted flowers, but the most distinctive feature is the strawberry itself. These fruits resemble cultivated strawberries except that they are smaller. The fruits have an excellent flavor. A few other plants also have rosettes of coarsely toothed compound leaves. However, the shape of the leaflets, the fact that there are always only the three leaflets, and the presence of runners is diagnostic for strawberry plants. The plants are found in old fields and weedy areas.

Strawberries are ripe from the end of May through mid-June. Fruitings vary from year to year and with the locality. Leaves for tea can be collected any time of year (even in winter), but seem to have their best flavor when the plants are in blossom. Wild strawberries are delicious raw, in pies, jams, jellies, and juice. Make a festive punch by soaking berries for several hours in wine; add more wine or champagne and a pinch of sugar just before serving.

Strawberry leaves for tea are dried indoors in a single layer on newspaper until crinkly dry (about 24 hours). Store the dried leaves in an air tight jar. To make tea, add a small handful of dried leaves to one quart of cold water. Bring almost to a boil and steep for ten minutes. Serve with honey.

Sumac, *Rhus spp.*
Cashew Family (Anacardiaceae)

These are clone forming shrubs which may cover large areas. They rarely exceed 20 feet in height and have an upward spreading growth form. The leaves are large (8"-16"), compound (10-30 leaflets), and alternate. The bright red fruits are borne in conspicuous tightly packed clusters that point up. The plants frequently occur in old fields and waste ground. It is impossible to confuse the edible sumacs with poison sumac, a plant which causes a dermatitis similar to that caused by poison ivy. Poison sumac, in contrast to the edible sumacs, grows in bogs and swamps and has white berry-like fruits which hang down in an open cluster.

Figure 34. Sumac: 1) Habit of a sumac clone (Ed Rutz); 2) Growth aspect; 3) Mature fruit, ready to cook; 4) Leaflets and fruit.

The red berried sumacs make a good tea as well as a pleasant cold drink (sometimes called Rhus-ade). Although any of the red-berried species are good, the hairy staghorn sumac has the best flavor.

Be certain that the berries are fully ripe (completely red) or they will not sweeten properly. The berries are used throughout the winter, although they become quite "ratty" by spring. Collecting the berries does no harm to the plant since sumac spreads underground (clonally).

Collect the heads of berries by snapping them off with your fingers or by cutting with a knife or clippers. Discard any stem which may have remained. Rinse well and place in cold water. To make a drink, one of two methods can be followed. Soak a number of heads in cold water for one hour and pound them well to release the flavor. Pour through a clean towel or cheese cloth to get rid of the hairs and then sweeten with honey or sugar. The other method (which does not require as many berries) is to place the berries in cold water and bring almost to a boil. Do not boil as it

EDIBLE WILD PLANTS

makes the tea bitter. Steep for ten minutes or until a dusky pink. Pour through a towel or cheese cloth and sweeten with honey or sugar. Serve either hot or cold.

The red heads can be hung in bunches to dry, strung on a string, or frozen "as is."

Figure 35. Walnuts: 1) Walnut tree growth aspect (Marguerite Bruce); 2) Fruit and leaflets; 3) Chambered pith; 4) Butternut (left) and walnut (right) mature fruits; 5) Leaf scars and buds; 6) Collected walnuts, ready to prepare; 7) Nut meats, ready to eat.

Walnuts and butternuts, *Juglans cinerea* and *J. nigra*
Walnut Family (Juglandaceae)

The walnut and butternut are related to the hickories, have alternate compound leaves, and are restricted to the lower part of our range. They are large trees with yellowish green foliage. The husks have a distinctive odor which smells somewhat like furniture polish or tannic acid. Some of the largest black walnuts grow in flood plains, but they also grow along moist roadsides and are frequently planted as yard trees. Butternuts also like rich, moist soil, but do also grow in dry areas. Aside from the odor, a very distinctive feature can be observed by cutting longitudinally through a portion of a young twig so as to reveal the central pith. This pith is highly diaphragmed and appears ladder-like in longitudinal section. The butternut is distinguished from the black walnut primarily by the more oblong fruit and the somewhat softer husk and shell.

Gather the nuts in late autumn after they have fallen from the trees. Squirrels use the nuts extensively, thereby helping themselves, as well as planting new trees by forgetting some of the nuts they buried.

The green outer husk of the nut is difficult to remove—it can be taken off with a hammer or by running something heavy (such as a car) over the nuts. The green husks have a pleasant smell, but will stain your hands a light brown. After removing the husk, the nuts should be dried for several months before cracking them.

To crack the nuts, use a vise, or a heavy nut cracker. A friend of ours uses a bandsaw very effectively, but most of us find that makes eating wild plants a little more exciting than we had anticipated.

Walnuts and butternuts are excellent raw or cooked in cakes and cookies. Butternuts have a distinctive flavor and are a little stronger in taste than the walnuts. We like them both.

Watercress, *Nasturtium officinale*
Mustard Family (Cruciferae)

This herbaceous perennial of shallow, slowly moving water can easily be recognized by its compound leaves bearing rounded leaflets, its soft succulent stems which frequently bear white roots near the points of leaf attachment, and its rather pungent odor when bruised. The flowers occur in white clusters during late summer and early fall. It may be found during the winter when it will be mostly submerged. In the summer, the shoots may reach as high as two feet. Its flowers are typical of mustards in that they are four parted, resembling a cross.

Watercress transplants very easily. Pull up a handful of the plants,

EDIBLE WILD PLANTS

Figure 36. Watercress: 1) Growth pattern of watercress with flowers; 2) Leaves and flowers; 3) Leaves and rootlets; 4) Collecting watercress.

being certain to include some of the white rootlets. Place the plants in another stream, weight them down with a rock, and they soon become established, usually in several weeks.

Collect the watercress by hand (or with a rake or a cane if the cress is hard to reach from the bank). Unfortunately, watercress seems to be affected by pollutants and since most of the water where you collect the plants will be contaminated, it is necessary to process the cress before eating. Unless you are certain that the water is not polluted, soak the cress in a solution of 1 teaspoon Clorox per 1 quart of water or in a double strength water purifying tablet solution for 20 minutes. Rinse well in several batches of cold water before using.

The leaves and young stems are excellent in salads, sandwiches or in soups. Since they are quite strong, taste carefully before serving.

To preserve, boil the leaves and young stems for two minutes, drain, pat dry, label and freeze.

58　　　　　　　　　EDIBLE WILD PLANTS

Figure 37. Wild ginger: 1) Leaves of wild ginger; 2) Flowers and leaves in a typical growth pattern; 3) Stems and unopened buds.

Wild ginger, *Asarum canadense*
Dutchman's Pipe Family (Aristolochiaceae)

Wild ginger rhizomes (modified stems) lie along the surface of the ground, branching and spreading to form large colonies. Two large heart-shaped, velvety green leaves occur at the ends of the drab green rhizome branches. At ground level in the early spring, a dark purple flower will appear in the fork formed by these two heart-shaped leaves.

The rhizome of this perennial herb is unmistakable year around because of its distinctive ginger odor. The plant is frequently found in rich woods and along the flood plains of streams and rivers. It can be collected at any time of the year, although plants are difficult to locate in the winter. The flavor and fragrance remain strong and pleasant throughout the year. Three to four inch segments are easy to pull off as the rhizomes lie directly on the surface of the ground.

Although unrelated botanically to commercial ginger and ginger root, wild ginger has similar uses. A four inch segment may be added to any vegetable or chicken dish while it is cooking. Remove before serving. To make candy, cover cut segments with water and boil about an hour until almost tender; add the same amount of sugar as wild ginger and boil another half hour; cool; roll the segments in granulated sugar. To brew tea, add several four inch rhizome segments to one quart of cold water, bring to just under a boil, and steep for ten minutes; serve with honey.

Wild rice, *Zizania aquatica*
Grass Family (Gramineae)

Wild rice is a tall growing annual grass of shallow water areas. It is slim with a conical open inflorescence. The leaves are spreading and up to 2½ inches wide. The plant can form dense colonies with literally thousands of plants.

Wild rice begins to ripen near the end of August and continues into September. An added benefit of checking the wild rice areas is to see the many ducks and geese which feed on the ripe grains.

Wild rice is fun to collect. The best method is to do as the Indians did and use a canoe or a kayak. The plants grow so close together that a heavier boat sinks down too deeply to move easily. Most areas are inaccessible from the shore and too mushy for wading. Spread a sheet in the bottom of the canoe and use a rake or a cane to pull the plants over the boat. Shake the mature plants and the grains will fall into the sheet. The grains are easier to collect if the plants have been tied into sheaves before the grains ripen. Collecting does not harm the plants since many grains fall into the water to reproduce the next year.

It is difficult to remove the tenacious hull which protects the grains. Therefore, the grains should be first dried, preferably out doors for several days. Bring them in at night to prevent dampness. Finish drying by placing the grains in a low temperature oven with the door ajar or by putting them in a dryer for several hours over low heat. The hulls then open a bit more easily and the grains can be extracted. We have not yet found a very efficient method of grain removal.

To cook wild rice, rinse it well in several batches of cold water, add three times as much water as rice, and boil about 50 minutes. Salt to taste

60   *EDIBLE WILD PLANTS*

Figure 38. Wild rice: 1) Habitat of wild rice; 2) Flower spike with ripe male pollen on the bottom and unripe female fruits on top; 3) Mature fruit with protective sheath; 4) Mature fruit ready for cooking.

and serve with butter. Wild rice is excellent plain as well as added to soups and casseroles.

Preserve by storing the grains with or without the hulls in airtight jars or freeze them.

EDIBLE WILD PLANTS

· Figure 39. Wintergreen: 1) General appearance of wintergreen, 4" high; 2) Leaf with notches; 3) Plant arrangement, showing rootlets, leaves, and mature fruit; 4) Mature fruit and leaves, ready for processing.

Wintergreen, *Gaultheria procumbens*
Heath Family (Ericaceae)

Wintergreen is a low, evergreen trailing plant which forms extensive clones in dry, open woods. Short upright branches (3"-4" high) with two or three alternate leaves occur at frequent intervals along the horizontal rhizome. The dark green, waxy leaves are obscurely toothed. The white flowers, which develop in midsummer, produce a bright red berry by early fall. These berries may remain on the plants throughout the winter. Take a few leaves, and crush or bruise them. This will yield an unmistakable odor of wintergreen.

To collect, cut off the leaves and red berries with a sharp knife, being careful to take only a small amount from each plant. The leaves need to be cut or bruised to exude the best flavor. The fastest method is to place the leaves and some cold water in a blender. Blend gently for one minute.

To make tea, place bruised or cut leaves in cold water to cover. Bring almost to a boil and steep for ten minutes. If a stronger tea is desired, steep the tea up to several hours. An excellent sherbet is made by substituting strong wintergreen tea for the liquid in a sherbet recipe.

The bright red berries are refreshing to eat raw; they also add a pleasant flavor and color to salads.

EDIBLE WILD PLANTS 63

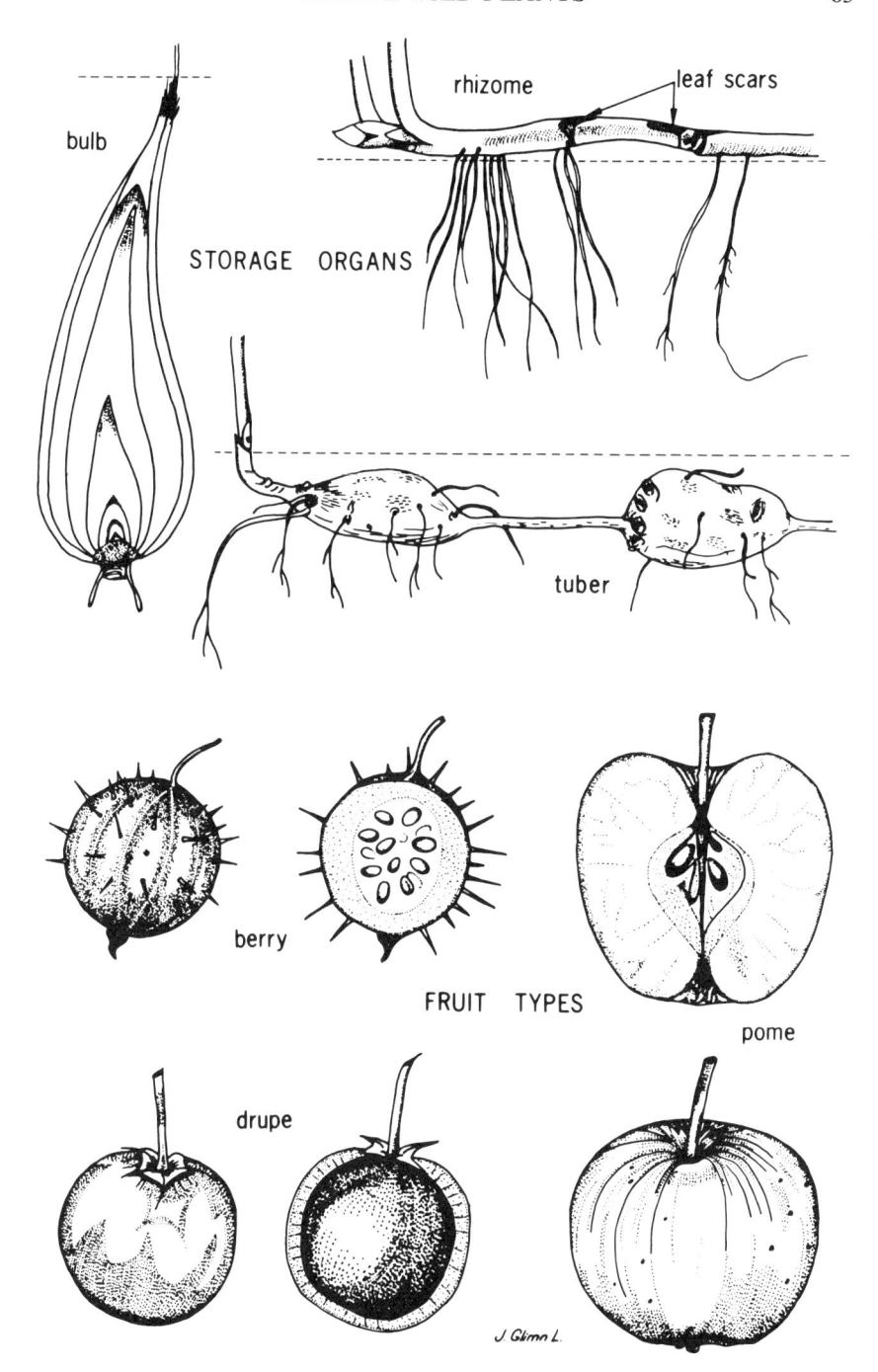

STORAGE ORGANS

bulb
rhizome
leaf scars
tuber

berry

FRUIT TYPES

pome

drupe

64 *EDIBLE WILD PLANTS*

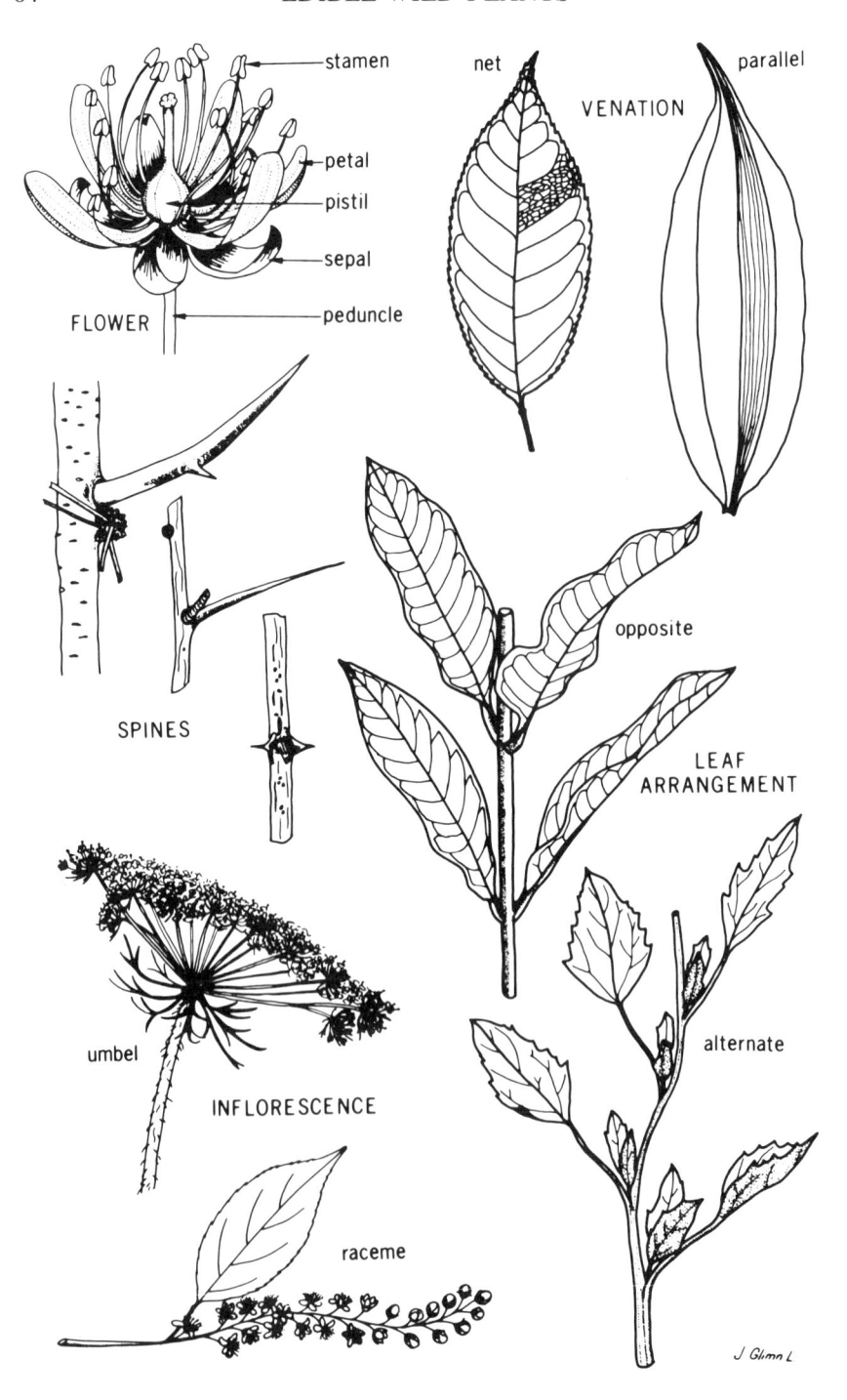

GLOSSARY

Alternate-having only a single leaf arise from that region of the stem—in contrast to opposite with two leaves arising from one region of the stem, or whorled with more than two leaves.

Annual-a plant which completes its life cycle in one year; that is, starting from seed, it will produce new seeds and die within a single year.

Axil-the juncture of the leaf with the stem, but only along the side towards the tip of the plant.

Basal-refers to leaves or structures located near the base or ground level of the plant.

Berry-a type of fruit with several seeds.

Blade-the flat light gathering or photosynthetic portion of a leaf.

Bog-a wet area, usually poorly or not drained and often acidic. They are peculiar for their unusual plants such as pitcher plants and orchids. Bogs are frequently characterized by an open central lake, a surrounding marshy mat, and an encircling ring of spruce and tamarack trees.

Bulb-a type of storage structure consisting of special leaves which are not green and often filled with starch, as found in onions.

Calyx-the outer protective "leaf-like" parts of a flower. They are usually green and often persist as the flower turns to fruit.

Clone-an aggregation of seemingly individual plants which are all genetically identical. They are organically connected by a common rootstock.

Compound-consisting of several parts.

Crozier-the young leaves of ferns which resemble fiddleheads as they emerge in the spring.

Cultivar-a plant selected by horticulturists and nurserymen and usually found only in cultivation.

Cyme-an arrangement of flowers into a flat topped cluster where the central flowers open first.

Diaphragm-a partition often occurring in a series, in the central portion of a stem. When the stem is cut longitudinally, there is a ladder-like appearance.

Drupe-a fleshy fruit with a single very hard protected seed, as in a cherry.

Elliptical-the shape of a leaf so that it is broadest at the middle.

Escapes-non-native plants which have managed to reproduce successfully out of cultivation.

Filiform-long and very slender, like a thread.

Frond-a large leaf, usually applied to leaves of ferns.

Fruit-the seeds and their protective or dispersal coverings.

Habitat-the kind of place where a plant is found.

Hardwoods-woods of deciduous trees (trees which lose their leaves in winter).

Herbs-plants which die back to ground level or totally die each year. They are usually soft bodied plants.

Inflorescence-a cluster of flowers.

Latex-a milky or gummy substance found in many plants when cut.

Leaf scars-the scar on the stem which is visible when a leaf falls in the autumn.

Lenticel-the small raised bumpy areas on the surface of young twigs, which allow the stem to breathe through its insulating bark.

Obovate-the shape of a leaf where it is broadest above the middle.

Opposite-the placement of leaves in pairs along the stem.

Ovate-the shape of a leaf so that it is broadest below the middle.

Palmate-the shape of a leaf, like a hand with approximately equal sized lobes going off like fingers.

EDIBLE WILD PLANTS

Peduncle-the stalk of a single flower or the stalk of a cluster of flowers.

Peltate-an attachment of leaves to leaf stalks when the stalk is not attached at the edge of the leaf, but on the lower surface.

Perennial-a plant which survives for more than two years.

Petals-the ephemeral, attractive parts of a flower.

Petiole-the leaf stalk which connects the stem to the blade of the leaf.

Photosynthetic area-the green, food producing regions of the plant.

Pollen-the dust-like, male-reproductive portion of the plant which is carried by wind, insects, or other pollinators.

Pubescent-hairy.

Range-the part of the world where the plant occurs.

Receptacle-the part of the flower to which all of the other parts are attached.

Rhizome-a stem which lies horizontally at or just below the ground's surface.

Rosette-a cluster of leaves arising from one point at ground level.

Sessile-a plant structure which sits next to the stem.

Sheath-a part of a leaf which encircles or sheathes the stem.

Shoot-a stem plus its attached leaves and buds.

Shrub-trees and shrubs blend together at some point, but usually shrubs are smaller and have several trunks.

Sinus-the little valley which separates the lobes of the leaf.

Spike-the arrangement of flowers into an elongate cluster with only a single central axis to which all the flowers attach.

Succulent-very fleshy plant tissues, usually because of a lot of internal water.

Swamp-a low wet wooded area which is drained because a stream or river passes through it.

Tap root-the main principal root.

Tendril-special plant organs which grasp other plants or things for support, often by coiling or gluing themselves on.

Terminal-at the end.

Tubers-swollen storage structures which grow as roots or stems underground.

Umbel-a type of arrangement of flowers where all the flower stalks appear to originate from one point.

Understory-the plants (herbs, shrubs, and small trees) which grow under the forest trees.

Urticating-stinging.

Edible Wild Plants of the Great Lakes Region
(Plants Arranged According to Usable Plant Parts)

I. Greens
  1. Asparagus
  2. Bracken fern
  3. Cat-tails
  4. Chickweed
  5. Dandelions
  6. Grape leaves
  7. Japanese knotweed
  8. Lamb's quarters
  9. Milkweed
  10. Nettles
  11. Onions
  12. Ostrich fern
  13. Pokeweed
  14. Purslane
  15. Sheep sorrel
  16. Watercress

II. Tubers
  1. Ground nuts
  2. Jerusalem artichokes

III. Teas and flavoring
  1. Catnip
  2. Beebalm, bergamot
  3. Blackberry, raspberry leaves
  4. Mint
  5. New Jersey tea
  6. Sassafras
  7. Spicebush
  8. Strawberry leaves
  9. Sumac
  10. Wild ginger
  11. Wintergreen

IV. Fruits, nuts, and grains
  1. Blueberries
  2. Blackberries
  3. Cranberries
  4. Elderberries
  5. Grapes
  6. Hazelnuts
  7. Hickory nuts
  8. High bush cranberries
  9. May apples
  10. Mulberries
  11. Pawpaws
  12. Raspberries
  13. Strawberries
  14. Walnuts (also butternuts)
  15. Wild rice

Cleaned wild leeks await a frying pan or a soup pot.

SIGNIFICANT NUTRITIONAL SOURCES IN WILD PLANTS

The plants are listed in descending order of nutritional values. "Grocery store" foods are in italics for comparison. For more details, consult in U.S. Government handbook on the *Composition of Foods*, public health departments, Euell Gibbons' books or current nutrition-oriented publications, such as "The Mother Earth News."

VITAMIN C
Strawberry leaves
High bush cranberries
Catnip leaves
Pokeweed shoots
Lamb's quarters
Watercress
Nettles
Strawberries
Oranges
Dandelion greens
Purslane

PROTEIN
Walnuts
Nettles
Lamb's quarters
Pokeweed shoots
Jerusalem artichokes (raw)
Watercress (raw)
Purslane
Oranges

VITAMIN A
Dandelions (cooked)
Lamb's quarters
Pokeweed (cooked)
Nettles
Elderberries
Purslane (cooked)
High bush cranberry
Lettuce

IRON
Purslane (raw)
Dandelion greens
Pokeweed shoots
Elderberries
Watercress
Lettuce
Purslane (cooked)
Lamb's quarters

CALCIUM
Lamb's quarters
Dandelion greens
Watercress
Purslane
Spinach
Pokeweed shoots

THE RECIPES

> Who doth ambition shun,
> And loves to live i' the sun,
> Seeking the food he eats,
> And pleas'd with what he gets.
>   "As You Like It"

EDIBLE WILD PLANTS

As one of our dedicated students said, upon reading through the manuscript, "These recipes all sound so good collected in one place! People will want to learn the wild plants just so they can try out all of these recipes!" We hope you will agree.

These recipes serve 4 people or more, depending upon the size of the people, how hungry they are, and the size of the rest of the meal. Most of the dessert recipes will serve twice that many. Some people will prefer to use honey (or maple syrup) instead of sugar. When not specified, use less honey than sugar; the results will tend to be a bit heavier and the food tends to burn more easily when using honey. Many people believe that honey and maple syrup taste better and are more healthy to digest. We have not had consistent results using honey in some of the baked goods or in the jam and jelly recipes.

We thank all of the many students and friends who shared their recipes with us and who were the testers of most of these ideas. A special thanks goes to Ellen's daughters, Anne and Julie, who both contributed much—from gathering to tasting to proof-reading—combined with great senses of humor. Lee Weatherbee has done the final seasonings for so many of the finished products. Brent Weatherbee always willingly ate any new dish, no matter how different the ingredients appeared.

We're always interested in your favorite plants and recipes. To send comments and/or to order more books, we repeat the address listed in the front of the book—Box 8253, Ann Arbor, MI 48107.

These simple cooking utensils are often mentioned in the recipe section and would be helpful to have in your kitchen.

blender
bowls, mixing (small, medium and large sizes)
canner, water-bath (optional)
casserole (oven proof)
cheesecloth
cookie sheet
dishes, baking (oven proof), 9" × 9" and 9" × 12"
egg beater
food mill
frying pan or skillet (made of good quality, heavy material)
jars, pint canning (optional)

jars, jelly (optional)
kettle, 8 quart capacity
knife, bread
knife, paring
mallet, wooden
measuring spoons, set of
muffin tins
pans, baking, 9" × 9", 8" × 12", 9" × 5", 9" × 13"
paper toweling
pastry cutter
pie plates (9" round)
saucepans with lids (stainless steel, enameled or other good quality material), small (1 quart capacity), medium (2 quart capacity), and large (4 quart capacity)
sieve
souffle dish
spatula, metal (or pancake turner)
spatula, rubber
spoons, set of wooden
tea kettle
wax paper

    Methods and ingredients have been kept as simple as possible, while striving for a gourmet touch. With humor and with love, we give you these recipes.

ASPARAGUS
(Asparagus officinalis)

COUNTRY-STYLE ASPARAGUS

Wash well; snap off and discard the tough ends of
- **1 pound of asparagus**

Peel the bottom several inches of the stem with a sharp knife or a vegetable peeler. Leave whole or chop in 1" pieces.
Bring to a boil
- **3 quarts water**
- **1 teaspoon salt**

Add the prepared asparagus and boil 8–12 minutes. Remove while still slightly crunchy. Drain and serve with
- **¼ cup butter or oleo, melted**

ASPARAGUS FRITTATA

Wash well, snap off and discard the tough ends of
- **1 pound of asparagus**

Peel the bottom several inches of the stem with a sharp knife or a vegetable peeler. Chop into 1" pieces.
Boil in a saucepan
- **2 quarts water**
- **1 teaspoon salt**

Add all asparagus except tips and boil 3 minutes. Add asparagus tips and boil 5 more minutes. Drain and set aside.
Prepare bread crumbs by crumbling in a blender
- **3 slices bread, whole wheat or white**

Combine in a mixing bowl and mix well
- **the prepared crumbs**
- **the asparagus**
- **2 beaten eggs**
- **1 cup Mozzarella cheese, diced**

Heat in a frying pan until very hot
- **3 tablespoons olive oil or cooking oil**

Pour in asparagus mixture and gently spread around. Cook until browned. Place a plate over the frittata and flip it over, sliding it back into the pan. Brown the second side and serve topped with
- **2 tablespoons parsley, chopped**

CHINESE ASPARAGUS SALAD

This simple-but-excellent recipe is adapted from the wonderful cookbook, Nutrition and Diet with Chinese Cooking, *by Christine Y.C. Liu, available from the author at P.O. Box 1332, Ann Arbor, MI 48104.*

Wash and remove tough ends from
- **1 pound asparagus**

Bring to a boil in a medium saucepan
- **2 quarts water**

Add the cleaned asparagus and boil 1 minute. Drain and plunge into cold water to stop further cooking. The spears will still be crunchy. Cut the asparagus on a diagonal in 1" lengths.
Mix the following ingredients in a small bowl
- **3 tablespoons soy sauce**
- **¼ teaspoon onion powder**
- **1 teaspoon seasame oil**
- **1 tablespoon cooking oil**
- **1 tablespoon vinegar**
- **⅛ teaspoon pepper**

Pour this mixture over the asparagus in a serving dish. Chill.

ASPARAGUS WITH CHICKEN OR TOFU FILLING

Wash and slice into 3" pieces, discarding tough bottoms
- **3 cups asparagus spears**

Boil in a saucepan
- **2 quarts water**
- **½ teaspoon salt**

Add asparagus pieces and cook 8 minutes. Drain and place in a buttered casserole.
Melt in a saucepan
- **4 tablespoons butter or oleo**

Add
- **4 tablespoons flour**

Gradually add
- **2 cups vegetable or chicken stock (homemade, canned or made from bouillon cubes)**

Stir until thick and smooth; simmer gently 10 minutes, stirring frequently.
Add

½ cup cream
¼ cup grated Parmesan cheese
(optional) 2 tablespoons sherry

Heat gently. Pour half of this mixture over asparagus. Top with

½ pound cooked chicken, sliced
or
½ pound tofu, sliced

Pour the remaining sauce over the chicken or tofu and place briefly under a broiler until lightly browned.

BLUEBERRIES
(Vaccinium angustifolium and V. corymbosum)

NORWEGIAN BLUEBERRY JUICE

This recipe was given to us by a Norwegian friend, Vegard Omdal.

Remove stems and crush

3 quarts blueberries

Combine in a large kettle

the berries
3 quarts of water
2 tablespoons vinegar

Boil for 12 minutes. Cool and let stand, covered, in a cool place for 24 hours. Pour through a sieve and sweeten to taste with

2–4 cups of sugar
or
1½–3 cups of honey

Heat to dissolve the sugar or honey. Chill well before serving.

BLUEBERRY JAM

Remove stems from

6 cups blueberries

Place in a large kettle and crush the berries with a wooden mallet. Measure 4 cups of crushed berries. Add to the kettle

the crushed berries
1 box Sure-Jell fruit pectin
2 tablespoons lemon juice

Bring to a boil, stirring constantly. Add

4 cups sugar

Return to a boil and boil hard 1 minute. Remove from heat. Let stand 2 minutes. Remove foam and pour jam into

hot, sterilized jelly jars

Cover with

paraffin, melted over hot water

BLUEBERRY MUFFINS

Sift into a medium mixing bowl

2 cups flour
2 teaspoons baking powder
¼ teaspoon salt
⅓ cup sugar
or
4 tablespoons honey

Add

1 cup blueberries

Combine in a small mixing bowl

1 egg, beaten
1 cup milk
4 tablespoons butter or oleo, melted

Add to the flour-blueberry mixture, stirring just enough to combine. Pour into greased muffin tins and bake at 400° for 20 minutes or until lightly browned. Serve hot with a plate of butter.

BLUEBERRY PIE

To make the crust, combine in a food processor (or a mixing bowl and a pastry cutter)

2 cups flour
¼ pound (1 stick) cold butter or oleo, cut into small pieces
¼ cup cold vegetable shortening
½ teaspoon salt

Blend 1 minute, or until butter/shortening particles are very finely cut. Place in a bowl and add

3–4 tablespoons ice water

Stir briefly with a fork, shape into 2 balls, and wrap in wax paper. Chill in refrigerator for 1 hour. Roll first ball ¼″

thick to fit the bottom of the pie pan. To make the filling, combine in a large mixing bowl
> ¾–1 cup sugar, depending on tartness of the berries
> ⅛ teaspoon salt
> 5 tablespoons flour
> 5 cups blueberries, washed and stems removed
> 3 tablespoons butter or oleo, cut into small pieces

Pour filling into bottom crust. Roll second ball of dough to slightly larger than pie pan size. Moisten the lower crust edges with water and adjust top crust. Crimp down with fingers or a knife so that the 2 crusts stick together. Slash holes in the top, so that steam can escape. Bake at 450° for 10 minutes, then at 350° for 30 minutes, or until pie filling is set and top is lightly browned.

BLUEBERRY PANCAKES

The epitome of gourmet wild foods.

In a medium mixing bowl, beat until foamy
> 3 eggs

Add
> 2 cups buttermilk
> ¾ teaspoon baking soda
> 4 tablespoons butter or oleo, melted

Sift in
> 2¼ cups flour
> 1 teaspoon salt
> 1 tablespoon brown sugar
> or
> 1 teaspoon honey

Beat well and place in a pitcher. Cover and let stand in refrigerator at least 3 hours or overnight. Just before cooking, add and mix well
> 2 teaspoons baking powder

Combine in a small mixing bowl
> 1 tablespoon flour
> 1 cup blueberries

Pour into the pitcher and stir gently to combine. Fry the pancakes on a hot griddle lightly greased with
> 2 tablespoons fat (bacon fat or cooking oil)

Add more oil if necessary. Serve hot with
> a plate of butter or oleo
> a pitcher of maple syrup

BLUEBERRY BUCKLE

This recipe from the "Piscataquis Observer" in Maine is our most requested recipe.

Combine in a medium mixing bowl
> ¼ cup butter or oleo
> ¾ cup sugar
> or
> ½ cup honey

Add
> 1 egg
> ½ cup milk

Sift together on wax paper
> 1½ cups flour
> 2 teaspoons baking powder
> ½ teaspoon salt

Combine in a small mixing bowl
> 1½ cups blueberries
> ½ cup flour

Combine all ingredients in the mixing bowl and pour into a 9" × 9" pan. Combine in a small bowl
> ½ cup sugar
> ⅓ cup flour, sifted
> ¾ teaspoon cinnamon

Cut in with a pastry cutter or fingers
> ¼ cup (½ of one stick) butter or oleo

When the mixture resembles cornmeal, pour it over the ingredients in the pan and bake at 375° for 50 minutes or until the top is light browned.

CAT-TAILS
(Typha angustifolia and T. latifolia)

CAT-TAILS ORIENTAL

Remove tough outer portions of cat-tail shoots, leaving the tender inner portions, measuring

1 quart cat-tail cores

Cut into 2" pieces; set aside. Heat in a wok or skillet

3 tablespoons vegetable oil

Add

the cat-tail cores
2 thin slices ginger
   (wild or commercial)

Sauté, stirring constantly, for 1 minute. Combine in a small bowl

1 teaspoon cornstarch
2 tablespoons water

Pour over cat-tails and stir until slightly thickened, about 3 minutes. Remove ginger.

Just before serving, stir in

1 teaspoon sesame oil

PICKLED CAT-TAIL SHOOTS

These are good right away and even better if allowed to marinate for 48 hours in the refrigerator.

Remove tough outer portion of cat-tail shoots, leaving the tender inner cores, measuring

1½ quarts cat-tails, cleaned

Combine in a medium saucepan

1 cup water
2 cups vinegar
2 tablespoons sugar
1 teaspoon mixed pickling spices
1 teaspoon salt
½ teaspoon celery seed

Bring to a boil and simmer for 5 minutes.

Add

the prepared cat-tails
1 clove of garlic, sliced

Boil 1 minute, then chill in the liquid. Drain and serve cold.

BOILED CAT-TAIL SPIKES

A plain recipe, but it's plain good!

Remove the sheaths from

2 dozen male cat-tail spikes

Bring to a boil in a large saucepan

3 quarts water
1 teaspoon salt

Add the cat-tail spikes and boil until just tender, about 8 minutes. Drain. Serve hot with

4 tablespoons butter or oleo, drizzled over the top

CAT-TAIL POLLEN POUNDCAKE

A delicious recipe adapted from a neighbor, Barb Stockton.

Combine in a large mixing bowl

½ cup cat-tail pollen
1 8-ounce package cream cheese, softened to room temp.
½ cup butter or oleo
¼ cup white shortening
1½ cups sugar
1½ teaspoons vanilla

Beat with a wooden spoon until well blended. Add, one at a time, beating after each addition

4 eggs

Sift onto wax paper

2 cups cake flour
1½ teaspoons baking powder
½ teaspoon salt

Add flour mixture to the egg mixture and beat until blended. Pour into a 9" × 5" loaf pan and bake at 325° for 1 hour and 15 minutes. Cool in pan 5 minutes, then remove and cool.

CHICKWEED
(Stellaria media)

Raw Chickweed is good simply washed, cut into 1" pieces, and added raw to lettuce, spinach or potato salads.

CHICKWEED HOT AND SOUR SOUP

Combine in a large saucepan

2 quarts chicken stock
   (homemade, canned, or made from bouillon cubes)

4 cups chickweed, washed and cut into 1" pieces
½ pound tofu or chicken breast, cut into ¼" slices
2 tablespoons sherry (optional)
4 tablespoons tamari or soy sauce
¼ teaspoon black pepper, freshly ground

Boil 5 minutes.
Mix together in a small mixing bowl
¼ cup water
2 tablespoons cornstarch

Add to soup mixture and stir for 2 minutes.
Beat in a small mixing bowl
2 eggs

Add to the soup and stir for 2 more minutes. Top with
4 tablespoons green onions, chopped in ¼" pieces
1 teaspoon sesame oil

Serve hot.

CHICKWEED-CARROT SALAD

This recipe is from Ellen's mother, Wilma Gardner Elliott.

In a small saucepan, combine
1 egg, slightly beaten
¼ cup sugar
or
3 tablespoons honey
1 tablespoon flour
½ teaspoon salt
1 teaspoon mustard (Dijon style)

Add
¼ cup water
¼ cup vinegar

Mix well and cook, stirring occasionally, until thickened.
Whip in a small mixing bowl
½ cup heavy cream

Add
1 cup chickweed, chopped
2 cups carrots, chopped

Mix all ingredients and chill in a serving dish. Top with
½ cup nuts, chopped

WILTED CHICKWEED SALAD

Half way between a vegetable course and a salad course.

Cook in a heavy frying pan until crisp
6 slices bacon

Reserve the drippings and drain the bacon on paper toweling. Crumble the bacon into small pieces. Return drippings to the frying pan and add
½ cup onions (wild or domestic), sliced
¼ cup vinegar
¼ cup water
3 teaspoons sugar
or
1 teaspoon honey
⅛ teaspoon salt

Cook and stir until boiling. Place in a bowl
5 cups chickweed pieces, washed

Pour dressing over the top and serve while hot.

MAGIC CHICKWEED POTION
DO NOT EAT!

This recipe was given to us by an elementary school teacher who helps her students to make this ointment to "cure the community ills." Used for skin problems and wounds.

Mix in a 9" × 9" pan
1 pound chickweed, chopped
1½ pounds suet
2 ounces bee's wax

Cover and bake at 200° for 3 hours, stirring occasionally. Strain and store in small jars with a lid. External use only.

CRANBERRIES
(Vaccinium macrocarpon and V. oxycoccos)

CRANBERRY JUICE

In a medium saucepan, mix
- 4 cups cranberries
- 6 cups water

Cook until berries are soft. Place a sieve or a food mill over a medium sized mixing bowl and strain the cooked cranberries. Pour this liquid pulp back into the saucepan and add
- ⅔ cup of sugar

or
- ½ cup honey

Check for sweetness, then boil gently until sugar or honey is dissolved. Cool and add
- 2 tablespoons lemon juice, freshly squeezed
- ½ cup orange juice

Serve cold.

CRANBERRY-NUT BREAD

An old-fashioned recipe.

In a small saucepan combine
- 2 tablespoons butter or oleo
- juice of 1 orange, freshly squeezed
- the orange rind, finely grated
- scant ¾ cup water

Cook 2 minutes or until butter is melted.
In a small bowl combine
- 1 egg
- 1 cup sugar

or
- ⅔ cup honey
- 1 cup cranberries, chopped coarsely
- ½ cup walnuts, chopped coarsely

Beat well and stir into the orange mixture.
Sift together onto wax paper
- 2 cups flour
- ½ teaspoon salt
- ½ teaspoon baking soda

Combine all ingredients and pour into a buttered loaf pan (9" × 5"). Bake at 325° for 1 hour or until set and lightly browned. Cool and slice thinly. Serve with butter or creamed cheese.

CRANBERRY SHERBET

This recipe is from Ellen's grandmother, Carrie Smythe Gardner. This sherbet was always served at Thanksgiving and Christmas dinners. Serve either with the meal or as a dessert.

In a medium saucepan combine
- 1 pound cranberries
- 2½ cups water

Boil gently until the cranberry skins pop open. Put through a sieve or food mill, which has been placed over a medium sized mixing bowl. Return liquid and pulp to saucepan.
Add
- 2 cups sugar

or
- 1½ cups honey

Heat until sugar is dissolved.
In a small bowl mix
- ½ cup cold water
- 1 tablespoon gelatine
- ⅓ cup lemon juice, freshly squeezed

Add the gelatine mixture to the saucepan. Cook, stirring, for 2 more minutes. Cool. Freeze until partially set, remove from freezer, stir well; freeze until hard.

CRANBERRY PUDDING WITH NUTMEG SAUCE

An old-fashioned recipe given to us by Ellen's sister-in-law, Gail Weatherbee Lincoln, of Owl's Head, Maine.

To make the pudding, blend in a mixing bowl
- 1 cup sugar

or
- ⅔ cup honey
- 1 tablespoon butter or oleo

Sift together onto wax paper
- 2 cups flour

2 tablespoons baking powder

Add to sugar-butter mixture along with

1 cup milk
2 cups cranberries

Pour into a 9" × 9" pan and bake at 350° for ½ hour or until set and lightly browned on top.

To make the sauce, combine in a small saucepan

1 cup sugar
    or
⅔ cup honey
¼ teaspoon nutmeg, freshly ground
2 tablespoons flour
¼ teaspoon salt

Add

2 cups water

Cook over medium heat, stirring constantly, until mixture thickens. Remove from heat and add

1 tablespoon butter or oleo
1 tablespoon vinegar

Pour sauce over plump scoops of the cranberry pudding.

DANDELION
(Taraxacum officinale)

A friend from Maine has a special ritual which accompanies his first spring dandelion feed. After boiling the greens, he places them on a slice of bread, sprinkles the greens with lots of butter and vinegar, tops it with another slice of bread and turns the sandwich over. He then cuts the bread into 9 pieces and sits back in ecstasy to enjoy his concoction.

BOILED DANDELIONS

In a large kettle boil

3 quarts of water
1 tablespoon salt
½ teaspoon soda

Add

2 quarts dandelions (thoroughly cleaned young leaves, crowns, and unopened buds)

Boil 10 minutes. Drain and serve hot with

a plate of butter
a cruet of vinegar

SWEET AND SOUR DANDELIONS

Prepare dandelions as in "Boiled Dandelions" except for the final butter and vinegar. Set aside.

In a frying pan, fry

4 slices thick lean bacon

When bacon is crisp, crumble to bits and set aside. In the remaining drippings sauté until tender

1 medium onion (wild or domestic) chopped

In a small bowl mix

1 egg, slightly beaten
¼ cup brown sugar
¼ cup vinegar
¼ cup water

Pour over onion-bacon dripping mixture in skillet and heat until slightly thickened. Add to the greens and top with the bacon bits.

MARINATED DANDELION CROWNS

Boil in a medium saucepan

2 quarts water

Add

2 cups young dandelion leaves, crowns, and unopened buds

Boil 5 minutes. Drain and place in serving bowl.

Combine in a small mixing bowl

¼ cup salad oil
¼ cup vinegar
1–2 tablespoons sugar
    or
1–2 teaspoons honey
¼ teaspoon garlic salt
¼ teaspoon onion salt

Pour over dandelions and chill before serving.

DANDELIONS ORIENTAL

Many good Oriental cooks have adapted their recipes to locally available wild foods in the United States. This recipe was given to us by a Korean friend, Yun Hee Aiello.

In a medium saucepan boil
   2 quarts water
Add
   4 cups young dandelion leaves, crowns, and unopened buds
Boil 1 minute. Drain.
Mix in a small bowl
   1 teaspoon cornstarch
   2 tablespoons cold water
Add
   2 tablespoons Japanese miso (optional)
   1 tablespoon soy sauce
   1 tablespoon sesame oil
   2 pieces garlic, minced
Set aside. In a wok or skillet, heat
   2 tablespoons vegetable oil
Add dandelions and cook, stirring constantly, for 2 minutes. Pour the cornstarch mixture into the wok and stir until slightly thickened, about 3 minutes. Serve hot. Good served over
   boiled and buttered rice

ELDERBERRY
(Sambucus canadensis)

ELDERBERRY FLOWER TEA

Combine in a medium saucepan
   2 cups elderberry flowers, major stems removed and firmly packed
   2 quarts water
Bring almost to a boil and steep for 15 minutes. Strain out the flowers and serve the tea hot with
   a pitcher of honey

ELDERBERRY FLOWER FRITTERS

In a medium bowl beat lightly
   2 egg yolks
   3 tablespoons water
Fold in
   2 egg whites, stiffly beaten
   1½ cups elderberry flowers, major stems removed
Sift onto wax paper
   1 cup flour
   1 teaspoon baking powder
   2 tablespoons sugar
   ½ teaspoon salt
Add to the egg mixture. In a heavy pan, heat to 370°
   1 quart cooking oil
Drop the fritter mixture in by tablespoonfuls and fry until lightly browned. Drain on paper toweling and serve with
   a dish of powdered sugar

ELDERBERRY FLOWER SHERBET

Combine in a medium saucepan
   3 cups water
   1 cup sugar
      or
   ⅔ cup honey
   ¾ cup dried elderberry flowers
      or
   1 cup fresh elderberry flowers
Boil, stirring constantly, for 5 minutes. Strain out the flowers and discard them. Add to the liquid
   ¾ cup lemon juice, freshly squeezed
   2 tablespoons lemon rind, grated
Heat 5 minutes. Cool. Freeze until partially set, remove from freezer, stir well; freeze until hard.

MULLED ELDERBERRY JUICE

Combine in a medium saucepan
   3 cups elderberries
   1½ quarts water

1 tablespoon cinnamon
½ teaspoon nutmeg
½ teaspoon cloves

Simmer gently for 1 hour. Strain out the fruits and discard.
Add
    1¼ cups sugar
    or
    ¾ cup honey

Boil gently, stirring constantly, for 5 minutes or until sugar or honey is dissolved. Check for sweetness. Serve hot or chilled.

ELDERBERRY JELLY

Remove large stems from
    6 cups (3 pounds) ripe elderberries

Place them in a large kettle and crush the fruit thoroughly with a wooden mallet.
Add
    1 cup water

Simmer 15 minutes, stirring occasionally. Strain through cheesecloth and discard the spent fruit. Measure 3 cups of juice.
Add to the kettle
    the elderberry juice
    1 box Sure-Jell fruit pectin
    ¼ cup lemon juice

Bring to a boil, stirring constantly. Add
    4½ cups (2 pounds) sugar

Return to a boil and boil hard 1 minute. Remove from heat and let stand 2 minutes. Ladle off the foam and pour the liquid into
    hot, sterilized jelly jars
Cover with
    paraffin, melted over boiling water

ELDERBERRY-APPLE CRUMB PIE

In a medium mixing bowl combine
    3 cups tart apples, thinly sliced
    1 cup ripe elderberries, stems removed
    ¾ cup brown sugar
    or
    ½ cup maple syrup or honey
    ¾ teaspoon cinnamon
    1 cup sour cream

Mix well and place in casserole or soufflé dish.
To make the topping, combine in a small mixing bowl
    ½ cup sugar
    ⅓ cup flour
    1 teaspoon cinnamon

Work in with pastry cutter or fingers
    ¼ cup (½ a stick) butter or oleo

When mixture resembles corn meal, pour it over the top of the casserole. Pat gently to distribute evenly. Bake at 350° for 50 minutes, or until the top is lightly browned. Serve with
    cheese or vanilla ice cream

OLD GYPSY CURE
DO NOT EAT!

We enclose this old Romany cure for "almost any ill" in case myths are true.

Combine in a small saucepan
    1 ounce cuttings from the frog of a horse's hoof
    1 leek
    1 ounce elderberry bark
    4 ounces fat from a pig's kidney

Cook slowly, strain, and store in small jars. Apply to wounded areas four times a day. External use only.

GRAPES
(Vitis spp.)

GRAPE JUICE

Remove stems and wash thoroughly
    2 quarts wild grapes

Place them in a large kettle and cover with

4 quarts cold water

Bring to a boil and simmer gently until the grapes are tender. Let the juice drip through cheesecloth or a clean pillowcase. Juice will be clearest if the cloth is not squeezed, but more juice can be extracted with pressure.
Add

1½ cups sugar
or
1 cup honey

Bring to a gentle boil and boil until sugar or honey is dissolved. Check for sweetness. Serve well chilled.

GRAPE LEAF PRESERVATION

Gather in early summer when young and tender

about 100 grape leaves

Remove stems and gather into rolls of 20, tying with string.
In a large kettle combine

2 quarts water
½ cup pickling salt
(available as coarse Kosher salt)

Drop the bundles of grape leaves into the water and boil hard 2 minutes. Remove and either use immediately or place in

sterilized pint jars

covered with the water/salt liquid. Screw on lids and place in a canner with water covering the jars. Boil 20 minutes.

GRAPE LEAVES, STUFFED

A wild version of a Greek favorite.

In a heavy skillet, heat

3 tablespoons oil
(olive or vegetable oil)

Add

1 cup onions (wild or domestic) chopped

Cook, stirring frequently, until onions are almost soft, about 5 minutes. Add and stir for 2 minutes

½ cup white or brown rice
(optional) ½ cup nuts, chopped

Add

½ cup celery, diced
1½ cups water
¼ cup parsley, chopped
¼ teaspoon pepper, freshly ground

Cook until rice is tender, 15–25 minutes.
In a large kettle, boil

2 quarts water

Add

about 50 grape leaves (fresh or home-canned)

Boil for 1 minute. Drain and cool in cold water. Gently separate the leaves and fill with the rice mixture by making little packets, using 1 tablespoon of rice mixture per grape leaf. Place the stuffed leaves seamside down in a medium saucepan. Add

2 tablespoons olive oil
(or vegetable oil)
½ cup cold water

Boil gently for 1 hour. Keep at least ½" of water in the pan. Serve with the following lemon sauce:
To make the sauce, combine in a small bowl

1½ teaspoons cornstarch
1½ teaspoons cold water

In a saucepan boil

¾ cup water

Add the cornstarch mixture and boil 1 minute. Keep warm. In a medium bowl beat until light and fluffy

1 egg
1 egg yolk

Add

3 tablespoons lemon juice, freshly squeezed
½ teaspoon salt

Slowly add the warm cornstarch mixture to the egg-lemon mixture. Return to saucepan and heat almost to boiling, stirring constantly. Pour the sauce over the grape leaves or serve separately.

GRAPE JELLY

Remove large stems from
   7 cups grapes
Place them in a large kettle and crush the fruit with a wooden mallet. Add
   2 cups water
Cook and simmer 10 minutes, stirring occasionally. Pour fruit and juice through cheesecloth or clean pillowcase. Measure 5 cups juice and discard the spent fruit. Return the juice to the kettle and add
   1 box Sure-Jell fruit pectin
Bring to a boil and add
   8 cups sugar
Return to a boil and boil hard 1 minute, stirring constantly. Remove from heat and let stand 2 minutes. Ladle off foam and pour the liquid into
   hot, sterilized jelly jars
Cover with
   paraffin, melted over hot water

GROUND NUTS
(Apios americana)

DEEP-FRIED GROUND NUTS

Wash, peel and slice about ¼" thick
   2 cups of freshly dug ground nuts
Dry them well on paper toweling. Heat in a heavy saucepan until very hot (almost smoking)
   3 cups cooking oil
Add and cook ground nuts, a handful at a time, until browned, about 1½ to 2 minutes. Drain on paper toweling while cooking the next batch. Serve hot as an appetizer.

SAUTÉED GROUND NUTS

Wash, peel and slice about ¼" thick
   2 cups of freshly dug ground nuts
Melt in a frying pan
   3 tablespoons oil
   (bacon fat or cooking oil)
   1 tablespoon butter or oleo
Add ground nuts and cook until just tender, about 8–10 minutes. Season with
   salt and pepper to taste
Serve hot, covered with
   (optional) 2 tablespoons parsley, chopped

DEVILED GROUND NUTS

Prepare ground nuts, as in the above Sautéed Ground Nuts recipe.
Keep them warm in a serving dish.
In a small saucepan, combine
   2 tablespoons butter or oleo
   1 teaspoon prepared mustard
   1 teaspoon vinegar
   dash of cayenne pepper or paprika
Simmer the sauce several minutes, stirring occasionally, and pour over the sautéed tubers.

HAZELNUTS
(Corylus americana and *C. cornuta)*

HAZELNUT APPETIZER

Heat in a heavy frying pan
   ½ cup butter or oleo
   1 tablespoon olive or cooking oil
Add and stir a few minutes with a wooden spoon
   3 cups of hazelnut pieces
Continue cooking and stirring until golden brown.
Add
   (optional) 1 tablespoon coarse salt
Serve hot or at room temperature.

HAZELNUT SOUFFLÉ

In a mixing bowl beat until light
- 3 egg yolks

Add slowly and beat with a wooden spoon
- 3 tablespoons flour
- 3 tablespoons sugar
- pinch of salt

Grind until fine
- ¾ cup of hazelnuts

Combine the nuts in a saucepan with
- 1 cup milk, warmed

Add the egg mixture and cook gently over low heat until slightly thickened. Remove from heat and stir in
- 3 tablespoons butter or oleo

Cool. Beat until stiff
- 3 egg whites

Fold (lift gently with an upward sweep) the egg whites into the cooled saucepan mixture. Place in a buttered soufflé dish or straight-sided casserole dish and bake at 350° about ½ hour, or until lightly brown. Serve hot or cold, plain or with a mixture of
- ½ pint heavy cream, whipped to form stiff peaks
- ½ teaspoon vanilla

HAZELNUT-CUCUMBER SALAD

Peel and slice into a serving bowl
- 2 cucumbers

Add
- 1 cup sour cream
- ¼ cup yogurt or cottage cheese, sieved
- 2 cloves of garlic, minced
- ¼ cup onions, minced (wild or domestic)
- ½ teaspoon salt
- ¼ cup parsley, chopped
- 1 teaspoon dill, chopped (fresh or dried)

Chill well and serve topped with
- 1 cup hazelnut pieces

EUGENE B. ELLIOTT'S HAZELNUT COOKIES

Named for Ellen's dad, who never cooked anything, but who loved these cookies.

In a medium bowl, blend with a wooden spoon
- 1 cup white shortening
- 1 cup sugar

Add
- 1 egg, slightly beaten

Mix together in a small bowl
- 1 cup sour cream
- 1 teaspoon baking soda

Add to the shortening-sugar mixture. Add also
- ½ teaspoon salt
- ¾ teaspoon vanilla
- ¼ teaspoon nutmeg, freshly ground
- 2¾ cups sifted flour
- ¼ cup ground hazelnuts

Mix well and chill in refrigerator for 1 hour. Roll ¼" to ½" thick (we like them fat), cut with a scalloped cookie cutter and place on a lightly greased cookie sheet. Bake at 350° for 10–12 minutes. Place on top of the cookies, either before or just after cooking,
- ½ cup hazelnuts, coarsely chopped

JAN BRUCE'S HAZELNUT CAKE

This excellent recipe is from Jim's mother and has been popular at many family and social events.

Sift together three times and place in a large mixing bowl
- 3 cups flour
- ½ teaspoon salt
- ½ teaspoon baking powder

Add
- 1⅓ cup soft butter or shortening (or a combination)
- 3 cups sugar
- ¾ cup milk

Beat for 5 minutes, or until well mixed. Add
- ¼ cup milk
- 1 tablespoon vanilla
- (optional) 1 tablespoon rum or brandy
- 5 eggs
- 1 cup hazelnuts, broken into small pieces

Beat until well blended. Pour into a greased and lightly floured tube pan. Bake 1½ hours at 350° or until lightly browned and a toothpick comes out clean. Serve plain or topped with the following frosting.

CARAMEL FROSTING WITH HAZELNUTS

A "good and simple" recipe from Jim's mom.

In a medium saucepan, bring to a boil
- 1 cup brown sugar
- 5 tablespoons butter or oleo

Add
- ¼ cup milk

Boil 3 minutes; remove from heat and cool.

Add
- 1½ cups confectioner's sugar
- 1 cup hazelnuts, broken into small pieces

Beat together until smooth and spread on a cooled cake.

HICKORY NUTS
(Carya ovalis and C. ovata)

CREAM OF NUT SOUP

In a large, heavy saucepan, sauté (lightly fry) for 4 minutes
- ¼ cup butter or oleo
- ¼ cup onion, chopped fine (wild or domestic)
- 2 stalks of celery, chopped fine

Stir in
- 2 tablespoons flour

Cook 3 minutes, stirring constantly. Add slowly
- 2 quarts of chicken stock (homemade, canned, or made with bouillon cubes)

Stir until smooth and simmer a few minutes.

In a blender, mix for 1 minute or until smooth
- 2 cups hickory nuts
- 2 tablespoons oil (peanut or safflower)

Add the blended nuts to the chicken stock mixture and simmer just under a boil for a few minutes, stirring frequently. Serve hot or cold and garnished with
- ½ cup nut pieces, chopped

HICKORY NUT DRESSING FOR SALADS

In a blender, pulverize enough hickory nuts to make
- 4 tablespoons of ground hickory nuts

Add
- ¼ cup olive oil or safflower oil
- ½ teaspoon salt
- ¾ teaspoon paprika
- ¼ cup lemon juice
- ½ teaspoon honey

Blend ½ minute or until smooth. Good served on
- lettuce, spinach or fruit salads

APPLE-HICKORY NUT SQUARES

One of our students gave us this delicious recipe.

Combine in a mixing bowl

2 cups sifted flour
2 cups packed brown sugar
½ cup butter or soft vegetable shortening
1 cup hickory nuts, chopped

Press the mixture in the bottom of a 13" × 9 " pan. Set aside.
In a mixing bowl combine
1½ teaspoons cinnamon
1 teaspoon baking soda
½ teaspoon salt
1 teaspoon vanilla
1 cup sour cream
1 egg, slightly beaten

Blend well with wooden spoon and add
2 cups of apples, peeled, cored, and chopped into small pieces.

Spoon the apple mixture evenly over the crumb base in the pan. Bake for about 35 minutes at 350° until golden brown. Cool before serving. Can be served plain or with a topping of
1 cup whipped cream, beaten until stiff

and flavored with
2 teaspoons honey

HICKORY NUT PIE

To make the pie crust, mix together in a mixing bowl with a pastry cutter or fingers until the mixture resembles corn meal
1½ cups flour
1 stick cold butter or oleo
3 tablespoons cold white vegetable shortening

Combine in a small separate bowl
3–4 tablespoons ice water
½ teaspoon salt
⅛ teaspoon sugar

Pour the water mixture into the flour mixture and mix together quickly with a fork. Turn onto a floured pastry cloth or a clean floured towel and blend the ingredients together with floured hands for 1 minute. Pat into a ball and chill, if possible. Roll to a round ⅛" thick. Put in pie pan, prick the bottom (to keep from puffing too much) and bake at 425° for 6 minutes. Cool slightly.
To prepare the filling, mix in a mixing bowl
3 eggs, lightly beaten
½ cup brown sugar
½ teaspoon vanilla
1 cup light corn syrup
¼ teaspoon salt
1 cup hickory nuts, coarsely chopped

Pour the mixture into the pie crust and bake at 350° for 45 minutes. Chill and top with
½ cup heavy cream, whipped

CARAMEL PRALINES

This southern recipe from Jim's aunt, Beverly Floyd, is sure to please those with a sugar sweet tooth.

In a heavy saucepan, bring to a boil, stirring occasionally
2 cups sugar
1 cup canned milk
3 tablespoons butter or oleo
⅛ teaspoon salt

Continue cooking over low heat for 10 minutes, stirring occasionally.
In a small heavy frying pan, place
1 additional cup of sugar

Heat and stir until caramelized (will be slightly liquid and brown in color). Stir slowly into first mixture. Cook until 236° (doesn't take long). Cool slightly, then stir in
2 cups hickory nut pieces
2 teaspoons vanilla

Beat until creamy and mixture loses its gloss. Drop from spoon onto waxed paper to form 3" patties. Cool until firm. To store, wrap in waxed paper.

HIGH BUSH CRANBERRY
(Viburnum trilobum)

HIGH BUSH CRANBERRY JUICE

Remove stems and wash
> 1 quart high bush cranberries, collected any time after the first hard frost in the fall

Combine in a medium saucepan
> the cleaned berries
> 2½ quarts water
> 2 1" pieces of orange peel

Boil gently for 20 minutes or until berries are soft. Let the mixture drip through cheesecloth or a clean pillowcase. Juice will be clearest if the cloth is not squeezed, but more juice can be extracted with pressure. Return to saucepan and add
> ½ cup honey

Boil gently 5 minutes, check for sweetness. Can be diluted with hot water or hot tea.

HIGH BUSH CRANBERRY PIE

Make a graham cracker crust as in the "May Apple Chiffon Pie" recipe, (see p. 95). Set aside.
Remove stems and wash
> 2 cups high bush cranberries, collected any time after the first hard frost in the fall

In a medium saucepan combine
> the cleaned berries
> ½ cup water
> 2 1" pieces of orange peel

Boil until berries are soft, then add
> ¾ cup sugar

Reheat to dissolve sugar. Force through a sieve or food mill. Measure 1 cup of purée.
Combine in a medium mixing bowl
> 1 package lemon-flavored gelatine
> ⅓ cup boiling water

Stir well to dissolve gelatine and add the berry purée. Chill in refrigerator until partially set, then stir briskly for 3 minutes. In a small bowl beat until soft peaks are formed
> 4 egg whites

Add
> ¼ cup sugar

Continue beating until stiff peaks are formed. Fold the beaten whites into the berry-gelatine mixture and pour into the graham cracker crust. Chill before serving. Can be frozen.

HIGH BUSH CRANBERRY JELLY

Make juice as in "High Bush Cranberry Juice" (above). Measure
> 4 cups high bush cranberry juice

Combine in a large kettle
> the juice
> 1 package Sure-Jell fruit pectin

Bring to a boil and add
> 5 cups sugar

Return to a boil and boil hard, stirring constantly, for 1 minute. Remove from heat, cool 2 minutes, skim off foam and ladle the jelly into
> hot, sterilized jelly jars

Seal with
> paraffin, melted over boiling water

This jelly is good on toast or biscuits. A favorite accompaniment is to tuck this beautiful colored jelly inside homemade Cream Puffs.

CREAM PUFFS

In a medium saucepan boil
> 1 cup water

Add
> ½ cup butter or oleo

When butter is melted add
> 1 cup flour, sifted

Stir vigorously and cook until mixture forms a mass which sticks together. Remove from heat and cool slightly.

Add 1 at a time, beating well after each addition
4 eggs
Beat until smooth and drop by heaping tablespoons on a greased cookie sheet. Bake at 450° for 15 minutes, then at 325° for 25 minutes. Fill with jelly.

JAPANESE KNOTWEED
(Polygonum cuspidatum)

BOILED JAPANESE KNOTWEED

Serve like applesauce.

Boil in a medium-sized saucepan
3 quarts water
½ teaspoon salt
Add
1 quart young knotweed stalks, washed and cut-up (remove skin, if tough, with a vegetable peeler)
Boil until just tender, 5–8 minutes. Drain and serve with
a pinch of brown sugar or
a dab of honey
4 tablespoons butter or oleo, melted

JAPANESE KNOTWEED JUICE

A refreshing drink tasting like a combination of rhubarb sauce and lemonade

Simmer together in a medium saucepan until soft
1 quart young knotweed stalks, washed and cut-up
3 quarts water
Force the mixture through a sieve or food mill, saving the juice.
Add
¼ cup honey or sugar
Mix well and taste for sweetness. Serve cold. Add
wild strawberries, if available

DEEP DISH JAPANESE KNOTWEED PIE

Prepare crumb topping. In a mixing bowl, combine
⅓ cup sugar
¾ teaspoon ground cinnamon
¾ cup flour
Cut in with fingers or pastry cutter
6 tablespoons butter or oleo
Set aside after mixing thoroughly.
To prepare filling, place in a medium saucepan
6 cups young knotweed stalks, coarsely chopped
2 cups apples, coarsely chopped
1½ cups water
Cook until tender and force through a sieve or food mill. To this mixture add
2 cups sugar
½ cup flour
½ cup sour cream
juice of 1 lemon, freshly squeezed
3 eggs, beaten
Pour into a buttered casserole and top with the crumb topping. Bake at 350° for 45 minutes or until nicely browned. Good served plain or with
(optional) ice cream or whipped cream

JAPANESE KNOTWEED FRUIT SALAD DRESSING

Steam together
4 cups knotweed shoots, washed and coarsely cut-up
1 cup water
Force through a sieve or food mill. Add
2 tablespoons butter or oleo
½ teaspoon honey or sugar
Combine in a saucepan
¼ cup cold water
1 envelope gelatine
Add
2 tablespoons honey
½ teaspoon salt
the purée
Heat gently to dissolve gelatine, then

chill well in the refrigerator. Spoon over
   apple chunks
and top with
   a handful of chopped nuts

JERUSALEM ARTICHOKE
(Helianthus tuberosus)

BOILED JERUSALEM ARTICHOKES

Scrub and remove skins from
   1½ quarts freshly dug Jerusalem artichoke tubers
Sprinkle with
   1 tablespoon lemon juice (to prevent discoloration)
In a saucepan bring to a boil
   2 cups water
Add the artichokes and cook until just tender, about 15 minutes. Do not overcook as they become mushy. Serve with a drizzle of
   ¼ cup butter or oleo, melted
   OR
place the cooked artichokes in a buttered casserole. Add
   2 tablespoons butter or oleo
   ½ teaspoon salt
   ¼ teaspoon ground pepper
   1 clove of garlic, crushed
   1 tablespoon parsley, chopped
   1 tablespoon onion, chopped (wild or domestic)
   ¾ cup heavy cream
Stir thoroughly and bake at 350° for ½ hour.

JERUSALEM ARTICHOKE APPETIZER WITH DIP

Scrub and remove skins from
   1 quart freshly dug Jerusalem artichoke tubers
Slice thinly or leave whole.
Sprinkle with
   1 tablespoon lemon juice (to prevent discoloration)
To make the dip, blend together in a small serving dish
   1 cup sour cream
   ¼ cup grated fresh horseradish
   ¼ teaspoon salt
   (optional) 1 teaspoon mint, finely chopped
To serve, place on a platter
   raw spinach or watercress
Pile the Jerusalem artichokes on top and accompany with the dip.

JERUSALEM ARTICHOKE PICKLES

An old-fashioned farmer's recipe.
Scrub
   1 gallon Jerusalem artichokes
Place them in a crock or large pan and cover with a brine made of
   1 gallon water
   1 cup of pickling salt (often available as coarse Kosher salt)
Let stand overnight in a cool place. The next day, mix in a saucepan
   2½ cups sugar
   1 clove of garlic, minced
   1 tablespoon turmeric
   3 tablespoons mixed whole spices
   2 quarts cider vinegar
Boil gently 20 minutes. Set aside. Rinse the tubers, drain them and pack them into
   sterilized pint canning jars
Reheat the saucepan mixture to boiling and pour over the tubers to within ½" of the top. Seal and process in a boiling water bath for 10 minutes. The pickles should mellow at least 3 weeks before serving.

JERUSALEM ARTICHOKE PANCAKES

Scrub and peel
   ½ pound Jerusalem artichokes

Place them in a bowl and add
- 1 tablespoon fresh lemon juice
- cold water to cover

Let stand at least ½ hour. Drain off the water, pat the tubers dry with paper toweling and grate them coarsely. There should be about two cups of ground artichokes.

In a bowl mix
- the artichokes
- 2 eggs, slightly beaten
- ½ teaspoon salt
- 1 small onion, chopped finely
- 1½ tablespoons flour
- ¼ teaspoon baking powder
- 1¼ teaspoons salt

Melt in a frying pan
- 2 tablespoons butter or oleo
- 1 tablespoon oil

Heat until almost smoking, then drop batter by tablespoonfuls into the hot oil. Turn when the first side is lightly browned. Add more oil as the batch progresses to keep the pan moist. Serve with
- applesauce or sour cream

JERUSALEM ARTICHOKE SALAD

In a wooden salad bowl, place
- 1 pound lamb's quarters or spinach, washed well and chopped into 1″ pieces
- ¼ cup onion (wild or domestic), thinly sliced
- 1 cup red cabbage, thinly sliced
- 1½ cups Jerusalem artichokes, thinly sliced
- 2 teaspoons lemon juice, freshly squeezed
- 3 oranges, peeled and thinly sliced
- 1 avocado, thinly sliced

Mix the following dressing ingredients in a blender or beat in a bowl with an egg beater
- ¼ cup onion (wild or domestic), finely chopped
- ½ teaspoon dry mustard
- ½ teaspoon paprika
- 3 tablespoons honey
- 3 tablespoons vinegar
- 1 tablespoon lemon juice
- ⅓ cup salad oil
- ¾ teaspoon salt
- 2 tablespoons parsley, chopped

Blend thoroughly and pour over salad.

LAMB'S QUARTERS (*Chenopodium album*)

BOILED LAMB'S QUARTERS

Wash well and cut into 2″ pieces
- 1 quart young, tender leaves of lamb's quarters

Bring to a boil in a saucepan
- 2 quarts water
- 1 teaspoon salt

Add the lamb's quarters and boil 5 minutes. Drain, check seasoning and add
- 2 tablespoons butter or oleo
- (optional) 3 slices of fried, crumbled bacon bits

CHEESE SOUP WITH LAMB'S QUARTERS

Melt in a large saucepan
- 3 tablespoons butter or oleo
- 1 tablespoon cooking oil (keeps the butter from burning)

Add and sauté (lightly fry) for 5 minutes
- 2 medium onions, chopped (wild or domestic)
- 2 medium carrots, chopped
- 3 stalks celery, chopped
- 1 medium potato, chopped

Add and boil gently for ½ hour
- 1½ quarts vegetable stock (the Swiss vegetable cubes are good)

In a separate saucepan melt
- 6 tablespoons butter

Add and stir until smooth
- 6 tablespoons whole wheat flour

Add several spoonfuls of the hot vegetable stock and blend well.
Combine all of the ingredients in the large saucepan and add
- 3 cups lamb's quarters (young leaves, washed and chopped into small pieces)
- 1½ pounds cheddar cheese, cut in coarse pieces
- 3 cups of milk
- 1 teaspoon basil (fresh, if possible)
- black pepper to taste
- (optional) 1 teaspoon tamari or soy sauce

Simmer for 10 minutes or until cheese is melted.

LAMB'S QUARTERS UNDER A CRUST

This recipe was given to us by a favorite gourmet cook who requests anonymity due to the inclusion of a pre-mixed ingredient.

Prepare according to the "Boiled Lamb's Quarters" recipe (above)
- 1 quart young, tender leaves of lamb's quarters

Drain but do not add butter. Set aside.
In a large mixing bowl combine
- 1 cup Bisquick
- ¼ cup milk
- 2 eggs
- ¼ cup onion, finely chopped (wild or domestic)

Beat the mixture about 20 strokes and spread in a shallow buttered casserole dish. Mix together in a mixing bowl
- the prepared lamb's quarters
- ½ cup Parmesan cheese, grated
- 4 ounces Monterey Jack cheese, cubed
- 1 12-ounce carton creamed cottage cheese
- ½ teaspoon salt
- 2 eggs

Spread over the batter in the casserole and bake 30 minutes at 375°. Let stand 5 minutes before serving.

LAMB'S QUARTERS QUICHE

To make the pie crust, mix together in a mixing bowl with a pastry cutter or fingers until the mixture resembles corn meal
- 1½ cups flour
- 1 stick cold butter or oleo
- 3 tablespoons cold white vegetable shortening

Beat together in a small separate bowl
- 3–4 tablespoons ice water
- ½ teaspoon salt
- ⅛ teaspoon sugar

Pour the water mixture into the flour mixture and mix together quickly with a fork. Turn onto a floured pastry cloth or a clean floured towel and blend the ingredients together with floured hands for 1 minute. Pat into a ball and chill, if possible. Roll to a round ⅛" thick. Put in pie pan, prick the bottom (to keep from puffing too much) and bake at 425° for 6 minutes. Cool slightly.

To make the filling, melt in a saucepan
- 2 tablespoons butter or oleo
- 1 tablespoon cooking oil

Add and stir with a wooden spoon
- 6 cups lamb's quarters, washed and chopped
- ¼ cup onions, chopped (domestic or wild)

Cook over low heat until tender, about 5 minutes. Set aside.
In a mixing bowl combine
- 3 eggs, beaten
- 1½ cups heavy cream
- ¼ cup Parmesan cheese, grated
- ¼ teaspoon salt

Beat together several minutes. Combine all the filling ingredients and pour into the partially baked crust. Bake in a 350° oven for 30 minutes or until puffed and nicely browned. A knife dipped in just off-center will come out clean. Let stand a few minutes before serving.

MAPLE (Acer spp.)

MAPLE SYRUP

In late winter when nights are still cold but daytime temperatures reach above freezing, tap
- **any species of maple tree**

Drill holes with a 7/16" bit to a depth of 1½–2" preferably over larger roots or under large branches, about 3' above the ground-snow level. Insert a spile (available at some hardware stores) or a hollow stick. Collect sap each day and process within hours of collecting to prevent spoilage. If not to be used immediately, keep sap very cold or freeze it. To process, bring sap to a rolling boil in a big pan, preferably outdoors due to the large amount of moisture which must be boiled off. Continue boiling until the liquid begins to thicken slightly. Over controlled heat on a stove, boil slowly until a candy thermometer reaches 219°. Pour through a filter made of layers of felt or flannel material. Store in a metal container (glass jars tend to break when the syrup crystallizes) in a freezer or refrigerator.

MAPLE SYRUP FRUIT TOPPING

Heat to boiling point
- **¼ cup maple syrup**

Cool slightly and add
- **3 egg yolks, beaten for 1 minute**

Heat again for 2 minutes, stirring constantly.
Cool and add
- **¼ teaspoon salt**
- **1 tablespoon fresh lemon juice**
- **¼ teaspoon ginger, powdered (wild or commercial)**
- **½ cup heavy cream, whipped to form soft peaks**

Pour over
- **wild or cultivated fruit, sliced**

MAPLE SYRUP AND BISCUITS

This recipe from Cindy Edwards was given to Ellen's daughter, Anne, on her 21st birthday, to insure a perfect reputation as a cook.

Combine in a mixing bowl
- **2 cups flour**
- **¾ teaspoon salt**
- **4 teaspoons baking powder**

Cut in with pastry cutter or fingers
- **4 very heaping tablespoons white shortening**

Add
- **¾ cup plus 1 tablespoon milk**

Stir just until combined and toss gently on a floured board for a few moments. Pat out the dough to ¾" thick and cut into rounds with a floured round cutter or a floured drinking glass top. Place the biscuits touching on a lightly greased cookie sheet. Bake for 10 minutes at 375°, until nicely browned. Serve with
- **a small plate of butter**
- **a pitcher of maple syrup**

MAPLE WALNUT ICE CREAM

Separate the yolks from the whites of
- **3 eggs**

Beat the egg yolks until light and place them in the top of a double boiler or in a heavy saucepan. Stir in gradually
- **1 cup maple syrup, slightly warmed**

Cook over hot water, stirring constantly, until the liquid leaves a thin film on a spoon (known as "coating a spoon").
Stir in
- **1 teaspoon vanilla**

Cool and fold in
- **3 egg whites, stiffly beaten**
- **1 cup heavy cream, whipped**

Chill in freezer for 1 hour; stir well, then add
- **1 cup walnuts or hickory nuts, chopped**

Freeze for 2 hours. Remove from freezer and stir the mixture well (improves the texture and mellows the ice cream). Return to freezer and freeze hard.

MAY APPLE
(Podophyllum peltatum)

Be certain that the fruit is fully ripe; it will be soft, yellow, and fragrant. Unripe Mayapple fruit and vegetation are poisonous.

MAY APPLE JUICE

Remove stem and blossom end of
> 2 quarts ripe, yellow May apples

Cover with
> cold water

Bring to a boil and simmer gently, stirring often until May apples are soft. Strain the mixture through a jelly bag or a clean pillowcase. Juice will be clear if the bag is not squeezed, but there will also be less juice. For more juice, squeeze the bag.
Add
> honey to taste
> sliced raspberries or strawberries (optional)

Serve chilled either plain or mixed with
> lemonade or white wine

MAY APPLE MARMALADE

Remove stem and blossom ends and cut into small chunks
> 2 quarts of ripe, yellow May apples

Add
> 1½ cups of water

Simmer gently, stirring frequently, until fruit is tender. Force through a sieve or a food mill.
Mix in a heavy pan
> 4 cups sieved May apple pulp
> 1 box Sure-Jell fruit pectin or other fruit pectin

Bring to a boil and add
> 5 cups of sugar

Boil hard, stirring constantly, for 1 minute. Remove from heat and let the mixture sit for 2 minutes. Skim off the foam and pour into
> half-pint jars, sterilized

Seal with
> paraffin, melted over hot water

MAY APPLE CHIFFON PIE

To make the graham-cracker crust, combine in a mixing bowl
> 1¼ cups fine graham-cracker crumbs
> ¼ cup sugar
> 6 tablespoons butter or oleo, melted

Mix and press firmly into a 8″ or 9″ square pan. Bake at 350° for 6 minutes. Cool.
To make the filling, remove stem and blossom ends of
> 1¼ quarts of ripe, yellow May apples

Cut them in small chunks and add in a saucepan
> ¾ cup water

Boil gently for 30 minutes, stirring occasionally. Add more water if necessary to keep from sticking and burning. Put the mixture through a food mill or force through a sieve. There should be one cup of pulp.
In a medium-sized saucepan, combine
> the May apple pulp
> 4 egg yolks, slightly beaten
> ⅓ cup of sugar
> 1 envelope unflavored gelatine
> ¼ teaspoon salt

Stir until mixture comes to a boil. Remove from heat and chill in refrigerator until slightly thickened.
Beat until soft peaks are formed
> 4 egg whites

Add
  ¼ cup sugar

Beat until stiff peaks form. Stir May apple mixture until smooth and fold in (stir gently with an uplifting motion) the egg whites. Pour into the graham-cracker crust. Chill in refrigerator until ready to serve.

MAY APPLE ICE CREAM

Remove stem and blossom ends from
  1¼ quarts of ripe, yellow
  May apples

Cut them in small chunks and add in a saucepan
  ¾ cup of water

Boil gently for 30 minutes, stirring occasionally. Add more water if necessary to keep from sticking and burning. Put the mixture through a food mill or force through a sieve. There should be one cup of pulp. Cool.
In a mixing bowl whip
  1 cup heavy cream
Add
  1 tablespoon lemon juice
  ⅔ cup sweetened condensed milk

Fold the cream mixture into the May apple mixture and freeze until partially solid. Remove from freezer and stir well, then refreeze until firm.

MAY APPLE HUMMINGBIRD CAKE

A favorite southern recipe from Marguerite Bruce.

Remove stem and blossom ends of
  2½ quarts of ripe, yellow
  May apples

Cut them in small chunks and add in a saucepan
  1½ cups of water
  the May apple chunks

Boil gently for 30 minutes, stirring occasionally. Add more water if necessary to keep from sticking and burning. Put the mixture through a food mill or force through a sieve. There should be two cups of pulp. Set aside.
In a medium bowl, combine
  3 cups flour, sifted
  2 cups sugar
  1 teaspoon salt
  1 teaspoon baking soda
  1 teaspoon cinnamon
Add
  3 eggs
  1½ cups cooking oil
  the reserved May apple pulp
  1 small can crushed pineapple, undrained
  1 cup walnuts, chopped

Pour into 3 cake pans (8" rounds) and bake at 325° for about 20 minutes. Cool and top with the following icing:
To make icing, place in a mixing bowl
  1 box powdered sugar
  ½ stick butter or oleo, softened at room temperature
  1 large package cream cheese, softened at room temperature
  enough milk to make the icing spreadable

Mix well and place on cooled cake. Top with
  ½–1 cup finely chopped nuts

MILKWEED
(Asclepias syriaca)

GENERAL PROCESSING

Use the same techniques with the young shoots, buds, and young pods, since all parts of milkweed are bitter when raw.

In a large saucepan boil
  3 quarts of water
Add
  1 quart of cleaned milkweed parts, cut into serving pieces

Boil hard for 1 minute; drain and repeat with fresh water 2 more times. Check

for bitterness, then proceed with a recipe below or serve hot with
   ¼ cup butter or oleo, melted and drizzled over the top

MILKWEED WITH A SAUCE OF MILKWEED

Cut and process as above in General Processing
   2 quarts of milkweed parts
After cooking, keep ¾ of the mixture hot and place the remaining ¼ in a blender. Blend (or force through a sieve or food mill) until smooth. Set aside. In a frying pan melt
   4 tablespoons butter or oleo
Mix in with a wooden spoon
   4 tablespoons flour
   ½ teaspoon salt
Add gradually
   1 cup of milk
   the puréed milkweed
Cook until thickened. Check seasoning and pour over the still warm cooked milkweed. Drizzle with
   ¼ cup of melted butter or oleo

PICKLED MILKWEED PODS

This is an adaptation of a tasty old-fashioned cucumber pickle recipe.

Prepare as in the general processing method above
   4 quarts of young milkweed pods
Combine in a large bowl or crock
   the processed pods of milkweed
   3 cloves of garlic, sliced
   ⅓ cup of pickling salt (often available as coarse Kosher salt)
Cover with
   cracked ice (cover ice cubes with a cloth or clean pillowcase and pound with a hammer or wooden mallet)
Mix well and let stand for 3 hours. Drain well.
Combine and boil the following

   5 cups sugar
   3 cups cider vinegar
   1½ teaspoons turmeric
   1½ teaspoons celery seeds
   2 tablespoons mustard seeds
Add the pods to the above mixture and return to a boil. Pour the mixture into
   hot pint jars
Seal and process in a boiling water bath for 5 minutes.

DILLY MILKWEED PODS

This is another good pickle recipe.

For each 3 pints of pickles, prepare as in the general processing method
   6 cups (3 pounds) of milkweed pods, both ends removed
Heat to boiling in a saucepan
   3 cups vinegar
   3 cups water
   ⅓ cup pickling salt (often available as coarse Kosher salt)
Boil 3 minutes and place pods in
   clean pint jars
Divide between the jars
   1½ teaspoons red pepper, crushed
   3 cloves garlic, sliced
   3 teaspoons dill seed
   3 heads of dill
Pour the boiling liquid and pods into the jars and fill to within ¾" of the top. Seal and process in a boiling water bath for 5 minutes.

MILKWEED TEMPURA

The seed silks inside the larger pods can be used for this recipe if the pods are still fresh and firm. Split open the pods, remove the seed silks (which will cling together inside each half). These are usually mild enough in flavor without additional processing.

Prepare as in the general processing method above
   2 quarts of seed silks, young milkweed pods or young shoots

Heat in a heavy pan to 360°
- **hot cooking oil to reach half full in the pan**

Beat together in a mixing bowl
- **1 cup sifted flour (part whole wheat is good)**
- **1 cup cold water**
- **1 egg, lightly beaten**
- **2 tablespoons cooking oil**
- **½ teaspoon sugar**
- **½ teaspoon salt**

Dip the pods or silks in the above batter and cook them in the deep fat until tender and browned. Drain on paper toweling. Serve with a sauce of
- **1½ tablespoons soy sauce**
- **¼ cup prepared mustard**
- **½ teaspoon wild ginger, minced**

MINTS (Mentha spp.)

MINT TEA

Rinse well and chop
- **1 cup fresh mint leaves**

Place in a saucepan and add
- **2 quarts cold water**

Bring almost to a boil and simmer for 10 minutes. Serve hot or cold. Sweeten, if desired, with
- **honey**

Mint tea can be poured into ice cube trays and frozen to use as mint-flavored ice cubes for iced mint tea, lemonade, and mint juleps.

MINT BREAKFAST DRINK

Both children and adults love this easy to make beverage.

Put in a blender
- **⅓ cup fresh mint leaves**
- **6 cups unsweetened pineapple juice**
- **1 banana**
- **(optional, but good and full of vitamins) ½ cup wild violet blossoms and leaves**
- **6 ice cubes**

Blend at high speed until frothy and smooth.

MINT JELLY

Crush or chop
- **1½ cups mint leaves and young stems**

Place in a saucepan and add
- **3¼ cups water**
- **(optional) ⅓ cup dry white wine**

Bring to a boil, remove from heat and let stand for 10 minutes. If the color absolutely disgusts you, add
- **several drops of green food coloring (optional)**

Strain the liquid through a jelly bag or several layers of cheesecloth. Measure 3 cups of the mint infusion and pour into a large saucepan. Add
- **1 package Sure-Jell fruit pectin**

Bring to a full boil, stirring constantly. Add
- **4 cups (1¾ pounds) sugar**

Return to a boil and boil hard 1 minute. Remove from heat, let sit 2 minutes. Skim off foam. Ladle into
- **hot, sterilized jelly jars**

Cover with
- **paraffin (melted over hot water)**

MINT TABOULI

Tabouli is a delicious Middle Eastern cold salad flavored with fresh mint; it is a favorite for after-field-trip lunches.

Combine in a serving bowl
- **1 cup bulghur wheat**
- **1½ cups boiling water**
- **1¼ teaspoons salt**

Cover and let stand for 20 minutes. Squeeze out water with fingers and add
- **¼ cup fresh lemon or lime juice**
- **1 clove of garlic, crushed**
- **½ cup chives or green onions, chopped**
- **¼ cup olive oil**

2 tablespoons mint, freshly chopped, or 1 tablespoon dried mint

Refrigerate 3 hours or more. Just before serving, add

1 tomato, chopped
1 cup parsley, chopped
(optional) ½ cup green pepper, black olives, or cucumber, chopped

Serve the tabouli as a separate salad course or as a cold main dish.

MINT CHICKEN

The touch of mint is a delightful addition to this southern recipe from Marguerite Bruce.

Grate onto wax paper
the peel of 1 large lime
Set aside the grated peel and squeeze the lime juice over
1 broiler-fryer chicken, cut in parts
In a small bag, mix together
½ cup flour
1½ teaspoons salt
½ teaspoon paprika
Add the chicken pieces and shake to coat each piece evenly. In a frying pan heat to almost smoking
¼ cup cooking oil
Add chicken pieces and brown them on both sides (will take about 10–15 minutes). Remove chicken and place in a shallow baking dish. Mix together
the reserved grated lime peel
2 tablespoons brown sugar
½ cup chicken broth
½ cup dry white wine (optional)
1 teaspoon fresh mint, chopped
Pour over chicken, cover, and bake at 375° for about 45 minutes, until tender (a fork can be inserted into the chicken with ease). Serve the pieces on a hot platter. Pour over the top any remaining sauce from the pan and top with
sprigs of fresh mint

MULBERRIES (Morus spp.)

MULBERRY SOUP

Mash in a food mill or in a sieve set over a medium-sized serving bowl
2 cups of mulberries, washed well (de-stemming is desirable but not necessary)
Add
½ cup sugar
½ cup sour cream
2 cups cold water
(optional) ½ cup red wine
Chill well and serve.

MULBERRY SAUCE

In a heavy medium-sized saucepan, cook together
1 pint mulberries, washed well (de-stemming is desirable but not necessary)
¾ cup of cold water
Boil gently, stirring constantly, until berries are tender. Force through a sieve or food mill.
Add
1 tablespoon butter or oleo
1 tablespoon honey or sugar
¼ teaspoon nutmeg
¼ teaspoon salt
Serve the sauce hot or cold with fish or game.

MULBERRY JAM

Wash (de-stemming is desirable but not necessary)
2 quarts of wild mulberries
Place them in a mixing bowl and crush throughly with a potato masher or a wooden spoon. Measure 5 cups of berries.
In a heavy large pan, place
the 5 cups of mulberry purée (smashed mulberries)

1 package of fruit pectin
(such as Sure-Jell)

Mix well and bring to a full boil over high heat, stirring constantly. Immediately stir in

7 cups of sugar

Return to a full boil and boil hard for 1 minute, stirring constantly. Remove from heat and let stand for 2 minutes. Remove foam and ladle immediately into

hot, sterilized jelly jars

Clean off the tops with a damp cloth and seal with

paraffin, melted over hot water

DOUG'S MULBERRY ICE CREAM

This excellent recipe was given to us by a favorite student, Doug Gosling, who is now an edible wild plants teacher and photographer in California.

In a medium bowl mix together and set aside

1 scant cup sugar
4 eggs, beaten slightly
¼ teaspoon salt

In a medium-sized saucepan, scald (heat until a thin skin forms on top)

1 quart milk or cream
(half and half is good)

Add ½ cup of the hot milk to the sugar-egg mixture. Stir well and add to the remaining milk in the saucepan. Cook over low heat, stirring often, until the mixture thickens and coats a spoon, about 15–20 minutes. Cool.

Mix together

2 cups mulberries, mashed
½ cup sugar
1 pint whipping cream
1 tablespoon vanilla

Add to the cooled saucepan mixture and freeze in a freezer or (even better) freeze in an ice cream maker. If frozen in a freezer, remove when partially set and stir well. This mellows the ice cream and improves the texture.

NETTLES (Urtica dioica)
BOILED NETTLES

Combine in a medium saucepan

3 quarts boiling water
1½ quarts young nettle tops, washed and chopped into ½" pieces
1 teaspoon salt

Boil until tender, about 10 minutes. Drain and place in a serving dish. Top with

4 tablespoons butter or oleo, melted
1 tablespoon lemon juice, freshly squeezed

NETTLE SOUFFLÉ

Combine in a medium saucepan

2 quarts boiling water
3 cups young nettle tops, washed and chopped into ½" pieces
½ teaspoon salt

Boil until tender, about 10 minutes. Drain well, pressing out excess liquid. Set nettles aside.

In a medium saucepan melt

3 tablespoons butter or oleo

Stir in

3 tablespoons flour

Add slowly

1 cup milk or light cream

Cook, stirring constantly, until mixture is thickened and smooth. Add

the drained nettles
4 egg yolks, slightly beaten

In a medium mixing bowl beat until stiff

4 egg whites

Fold the egg whites gradually into the saucepan mixture. Pour into a buttered soufflé dish and bake at 350° for ½ hour, or until puffed and lightly browned. Serve immediately.

NETTLE-CHICKEN SOUP

Combine in a medium saucepan

5 cups chicken broth

3 cups young nettle tops,
washed and chopped into ½"
pieces

Boil 10 minutes. For a smooth soup, force the cooked nettles through a sieve or food mill or blend 1 minute in a blender. Return nettles and liquid to the saucepan and add

3 tablespoons heavy cream or milk
1 tablespoon butter or oleo
½ teaspoon salt
¼ teaspoon pepper, freshly ground

Simmer briefly and serve.

NETTLE-LEEK SOUP

Combine in a large saucepan

4 cups potatoes, peeled and diced
3 cups leeks or onions, peeled
and sliced (wild or domestic)
2 quarts water
1 tablespoon salt

Boil gently until vegetables are tender, about 50 minutes. Force the mixture through a sieve or food mill. Return to a boil and add

1½ cups young nettle tops, washed
and chopped into ½" pieces
2 tablespoons butter or oleo

Boil until nettles are tender, about 10 more minutes and serve.

NETTLE YORKSHIRE PUDDING

This is a combination of two tasty traditional foods of Great Britain. Our students call it "Robin Hood's Pie."

Combine in a medium saucepan

2 quarts boiling water
1 quart young nettle tops, washed
and chopped into ½" pieces
½ teaspoon salt

Boil until tender, about 10 minutes. Drain well. Set aside. In a medium bowl beat until light

4 eggs

Stir in and then set aside:

the drained nettles
1½ cups milk

4 tablespoons butter or oleo, melted

Sift together

1½ cups flour
½ teaspoon salt
1¼ teaspoons baking powder

Stir the flour mixture into the egg/milk mixture. Beat 1 minute with an egg beater. Place in a greased 8"× 12" baking pan and bake at 350° for about 1 hour, or until lightly browned.

NETTLES IN GREEK FILO

This wonderful recipe is based on a traditional recipe for Greek spinach pastry. Filo dough can be purchased at grocery stores specializing in Middle Eastern foods. The dough can be kept frozen until 1 hour before using.

Thaw but keep covered with a slightly damp cloth when not in immediate use (to keep from drying out)

1 1-pound package of Greek
filo dough

Combine in a large saucepan

3 quarts boiling water
1½ quarts young nettle tops,
washed and chopped into
½" pieces
1 teaspoon salt

Boil until tender, about 10 minutes. Drain and set aside. In a frying pan melt

3 additional tablespoons butter
or oleo

Add and cook for 7–8 minutes, stirring occasionally

1 cup onions (wild or
domestic), chopped
½ teaspoon salt

When onions are tender add

the drained nettles
5 eggs, beaten slightly
2 cups feta cheese, crumbled
2 cups cottage cheese
½ teaspoon oregano
1 teaspoon basil (fresh, if possible)
½ cup pine nuts (optional,
but good)

Set aside.

In a small sauce pan, melt and keep warm
   ½ pound butter or oleo
Butter a 9″ × 13″ baking pan. Place in the pan
   1 filo sheet
Brush it with
   2 tablespoons of the melted butter
Continue placing filo and brushing it with butter until there are 8 layers. Add half of the nettle mixture and spread it evenly. Then continue with 8 more layers of filo, with melted butter between each layer. Add the remaining nettle mixture, spreading evenly. Continue to add 8 more filo layers, brushing with butter each time. Butter the top layer and bake uncovered for about 1 hour or until golden brown. Serve in fat squares hot or cold.

NEW JERSEY TEA
(Ceanothus americanus)

NEW JERSEY TEA, FRESH

Combine in a large saucepan
   1 small handful of New Jersey tea leaves (flowers, too, if they are available)
   2 quarts of cold water
Bring almost to a boil and simmer for 15 minutes. Strain out the leaves and flowers and serve with
   a pitcher of honey

NEW JERSEY TEA, DRIED

This tea tastes like Oriental tea, but with no caffeine.

Dry in a single layer on newspaper
   clean leaves of New Jersey tea (flowers, too, if available)
Dry until crinkly dry, usually about 24 hours. Store in jars with a screw lid, away from heat and light. To make tea, place in a large saucepan
   1 small handful of dried leaves
   2½ quarts of cold water
Bring almost to a boil and simmer for 15 minutes. Strain out the leaves and flowers and serve with
   a pitcher of honey

SPICED NEW JERSEY TEA

Combine in a large saucepan
   1 small handful of fresh or dried New Jersey tea leaves (and flowers, if available)
   2½ quarts of cold water
   1 teaspoon whole cloves
   1 small piece of cinnamon stick
   3 tablespoons honey
   juice of 1 lemon
   juice of 2 oranges
   (optional) ½ cup of dried blueberries
Bring almost to a boil and simmer 20 minutes. Strain out the leaves and the spices and serve hot.

ONIONS (Allium spp.)

Wild onions, wild garlic, and wild leeks each have their own distinctive flavor. Use them separately or combined in any of the following recipes. Many other wild recipes also call for wild onions, if available.

SAUTÉED ONIONS

Clean and chop into slices
   4 cups leeks or other wild onions
Melt in a frying pan
   4 tablespoons butter or oleo
   1 tablespoon cooking oil
Add the onions and cook 5 minutes or until just tender.
Top with
   (optional) ¼ cup Parmesan cheese

ONIONS IN CREAM SAUCE

Clean and chop into slices
- **4 cups leeks or other wild onions**

Melt in a frying pan
- **4 tablespoons butter or oleo**
- **1 tablespoon cooking oil**

Add the onions and cook 5 minutes or until just tender.

Add and mix well with a wooden spoon
- **2 tablespoons flour**

Stir in slowly
- **1 cup milk or vegetable stock, heated slightly**
- **¼ teaspoon salt**
- **(optional) 1 teaspoon sherry**

Cook and stir constantly until thickened, about 5 more minutes.

Add onions, correct seasoning, and serve hot. Delicious served over
- **(optional) boiled potatoes or buttered toast**

TRADITIONAL RAMP SOUP

This mountain recipe is from the Richwood, West Virginia Ramp Festival.

Boil in a large saucepan for 15 minutes
- **2 quarts salted water**
- **1 pound of beef**

Remove any scum which forms. Dice and add to the mixture
- **20 ramps (wild leeks)**
- **5 stalks celery**
- **3 carrots**
- **1 pound potatoes**

Simmer 2½ hours. Remove meat and keep warm.

In a frying pan, sauté for 10 minutes, or until tender
- **20 ramps**
- **4 tablespoons butter or oleo**

Add
- **1 cup of soup**

Simmer for 10 minutes. Put the two leek mixtures through a sieve or food mill and serve hot in a soup bowl, accompanied by the meat.

WILD ONION SOUP FRENCH STYLE

Melt in a heavy saucepan
- **3 tablespoons butter or oleo**
- **1 tablespoon olive oil or cooking oil**

Add
- **4 cups of ramps (wild leeks), thinly sliced**

Stir well and cover. Cook, stirring occasionally, until tender, about 15 minutes. Remove cover and add
- **¼ teaspoon sugar**
- **1 teaspoon salt**

Cook and stir with a wooden spoon until nicely browned.

Add and stir for 2 minutes
- **2 tablespoons flour**

Add slowly, while stirring with a wooden spoon
- **2 quarts of hot bouillon (beef or vegetable, homemade, canned, or made from bouillon cubes)**
- **½ cup Parmesan cheese**

Simmer gently for an hour or more. Five minutes before serving, add
- **(optional) 1 cup red wine**
- **1 bay leaf (wild or commercial)**
- **¼ teaspoon sage**
- **2 tablespoons parsley, chopped**
- **2 tablespoons chives, chopped**

Serve hot.

OSTRICH FERN
(Matteuccia struthiopteris)

BOILED OSTRICH FERN

Simple, but so good most people use only this method.

Wash, recut stem ends and remove brown fuzz from
- **2 quarts of fiddleheads**

Bring to a boil in a saucepan
- **1 quart water**
- **1 teaspoon salt**

Add the fiddleheads and boil until almost tender, about 8–12 minutes. Serve with
> 4 tablespoons butter or oleo, melted (optional) lemon slices or a cruet of vinegar

FIDDLEHEADS WITH HOLLANDAISE SAUCE

Wash, recut stem ends and remove brown fuzz from
> 2 quarts of fiddleheads

Bring to a boil in a saucepan
> 1 quart water
> 1 teaspoon salt

Add the fiddleheads and boil for 10 minutes. They will be slightly crisp. Drain and set aside; keep warm.
In a blender mix for ½ minute
> 3 egg yolks
> 2 tablespoons lemon juice
> ¼ teaspoon salt
> ¼ teaspoon pepper

Add slowly
> 1 stick (¼ pound) butter or oleo, melted

Place fiddleheads in a warmed serving dish and pour the sauce over the top.

MARINATED FIDDLEHEADS

Wash, recut stem ends and remove brown fuzz from
> 2 quarts of fiddleheads

Bring to a boil in a saucepan
> 3 tablespoons vinegar
> juice of 1 lemon
> 3 cups of water
> 1 clove of garlic, minced
> ½ cup of olive oil or salad oil
> 1 tablespoon parsley, chopped
> 1 teaspoon salt
> pinch of thyme
> 2 stalks celery, chopped finely
> ¼ teaspoon freshly ground pepper

Add the fiddleheads and cook until almost tender, about 10 minutes. Cool in the liquid. Serve chilled in a small amount of the liquid.

FIDDLEHEAD SOUP

Wash, recut stem ends and remove brown fuzz from
> 1 quart of fiddleheads

In a saucepan, bring to a boil
> 2½ quarts chicken broth (homemade, canned, or made from bouillon cubes)

Add the fiddleheads and boil 10 minutes.
Beat in a small mixing bowl until frothy
> 4 eggs

Add
> ½ cup lemon juice

Mix in 1 cup of hot chicken broth and mix well. Put all the ingredients in the saucepan and simmer gently 5 minutes. Top with
> ½ cup wild chives or green onions, chopped

PAWPAW (Asimina triloba)

TROPICAL PAWPAW PUNCH

Peel and remove seeds from
> 2 large (or 3 small) ripe pawpaws

Chop the pulp coarsely. Place in a blender with
> 1 cup milk
> 4 tablespoons fresh lime juice
> ¼ cup honey
> ½ teaspoon vanilla
> ⅔ cup crushed ice

Blend at high speed for about one minute or until smooth. Serve chilled.

PAWPAW YOGURT

Peel and remove seeds from
> 2 ripe pawpaws

Coarsely chop the pulp and put through a food mill or force through a sieve. There should be about 1 cup of pulp. Combine in a serving bowl
> the pawpaw pulp
> 3 cups plain yogurt

½ cup honey
¼ teaspoon nutmeg
¼ teaspoon cloves
1 teaspoon cinnamon

Served chilled or frozen, topped with
(optional) ¼ cup mint leaves, finely chopped

PAWPAW BREAD

Peel and remove seeds from
2 large (or 3 small) ripe pawpaws

Mash
1 ripe banana

Combine pawpaws and banana and force through a sieve or food mill. Place in a mixing bowl
the pawpaw-banana mixture
2 eggs, beaten

Sift together on wax paper
2 cups flour
⅔ cups sugar
½ teaspoon salt
1 teaspoon baking soda

Combine both mixtures. Stir in
(optional) ½ cup walnuts or hickory nuts, broken into pieces

Place in a greased 8" × 4" loaf pan and bake at 350° for about 1 hour, or until delicately browned and an inserted toothpick comes out clean. Serve with
a plate of butter or oleo

PAWPAW PUDDING OR PIE

Peel and remove seeds from
2 ripe pawpaws

Force through a sieve or food mill. There should be 1 cup of pulp. Set aside.
In a medium saucepan mix
½ cup brown sugar
1 envelope unflavored gelatine
½ teaspoon salt

Stir in
⅔ cup of milk
3 egg yolks, slightly beaten

Cook and stir constantly until the mixture boils. Remove from heat and stir in
the pawpaw pulp

Chill about 30 minutes.
Beat with an egg beater until soft peaks form
3 egg whites

Add gradually
¼ cup sugar

Continue beating until stiff peaks form. Fold egg white mixture into the partially set pawpaw mixture. Chill thoroughly and serve topped with
(optional) ½ cup hickory nuts or walnuts

or pour into a
cooked 9" pie crust or graham cracker crust

Keep chilled.

POKEWEED
(Phytolacca americana)

NEVER SERVE POKEWEED RAW

Even the famous poke sallet of the Southern states is cooked, due to a poisonous substance which is lessened by boiling. Proper processing renders the plant edible.

BOILED POKEWEED

This is the traditional Southern method.

In a large pan, boil
3 quarts water
1 teaspoon salt

Add
1 quart young poke stalks (under 8" tall), washed and cut into 2" lengths

Boil hard one minute. Drain well, discarding the water. Repeat at least twice, using fresh boiling water each time. In the last water, cook until tender. Drain and serve hot with

4 tablespoons butter or oleo, melted
a cruet of vinegar (optional, but traditional) 4 slices of cooked bacon, crumbled

PENNSYLVANIA DUTCH POKEWEED

This recipe was given to us by a member of our first class in the early 1970's.

In a frying pan, fry slowly
- 4 slices bacon

When bacon is crisp, remove from pan and place on paper toweling. Cook as directed in the "Boiled Pokeweed" recipe, except for the final 3 ingredients
- 1 quart young pokeweed shoots (under 8" tall), washed and cut into 2" lengths

Drain pokeweed well and place in a serving dish; set aside and keep warm.
Add to the remaining bacon fat in the frying pan
- 1 tablespoon honey
or
- ¼ cup sugar
- ½ teaspoon salt
- 1 tablespoon cornstarch
- 1 egg, beaten
- ¼ cup cider vinegar
- 1 cup milk or water

Cook for 5 minutes or until slightly thickened, stirring often. Pour over cooked pokeweed and top with crumbled bacon.

POKEWEED CHEESE SOUP

Melt in a frying pan
- 3 tablespoons butter or oleo
Add
- 2 medium onions, diced
or
- ½ cup wild onions, chopped
- 2 medium carrots, thinly sliced
- 3 stalks celery, coarsely chopped
- 1 medium potato, diced

Sauté 8 minutes. Place ingredients in a large pan and add
- 1½ quarts vegetable stock (homemade or bouillon cubes)

Bring to a boil and simmer ½ hour. Cook as directed in the "Boiled Pokeweed" recipe, except for the final 3 ingredients
- 3 cups young pokeweed shoots (under 8" tall), washed and cut into 1" lengths

Drain well and set aside.
In a medium-sized saucepan, melt
- 6 tablespoons butter or oleo
Mix in
- 6 tablespoons whole wheat flour

Stir until the mixture is smooth, 3–5 minutes. Add 1 cup of the vegetable stock and stir until well blended.
Add to the large pan along with
- 1½ pounds cheddar cheese, coarsely grated or chopped
- 3 cups milk
- the pre-cooked pokeweed
- 1 teaspoon fresh basil
or
- ½ teaspoon dried basil
- ½ teaspoon freshly ground black pepper
- (optional) 1 teaspoon tamari

Boil gently until cheese melts. Serve hot.

POKEWEED AU GRATIN

Cook as directed in the "Boiled Pokeweed" recipe, except for the final 3 ingredients
- 1 quart young pokeweed shoots (under 8" tall), washed and cut into 2" lengths

Drain well and set aside.
In a frying pan, melt
- 1 tablespoon butter or oleo
Add
- ½ cup onions (wild or domestic), chopped

Sauté until onions are tender.
Add and cook, stirring constantly, for 2 minutes

1 tablespoon flour

Gradually blend in with a wooden spoon

1½ cups milk or light cream

Simmer gently for 15 minutes, stirring often.

Add

1 cup cheddar cheese, grated

Mix well and pour over pokeshoots in the casserole.

Cover with

whole wheat bread crumbs (use a blender, if you have one)

Bake at 350° for 15 minutes or until lightly browned.

PURSLANE
(Portulaca oleracea)

RAW PURSLANE DIP

In a small serving bowl mix together

1 cup purslane, washed and chopped into ½" pieces

½ cup sour cream

¼ cup onion (wild or domestic), chopped

¼ teaspoon salt

(optional) 3 drops tabasco sauce

Chill in refrigerator at least an hour. Serve with

chips or crackers

AUSTRIAN SALAD

A wild adaptation of a tasty peasant salad from the Austrian Alps.

Mix in a serving bowl

2 cups purslane, washed and chopped into 1" pieces

1 large clove garlic, minced or put through a garlic press

Force through a sieve or a food mill

¾ cup cottage cheese

¼ cup sour cream

Add to the purslane mixture and season with

½ teaspoon salt

¼ teaspoon pepper, freshly ground

Check seasoning and chill for at least one hour. Serve plain or set in a bed of

lettuce and/or watercress

PURSLANE DILLS

A classic, easy farmer's pickle.

Have on hand

a plump head of garlic

a small jar of peppercorns

a small jar of cloves

a bunch of fresh dill (or a small jar of dill seed)

Wash and cut into 3" lengths

3 quarts purslane

Place them in

clean, sterilized pint jars

Add to each jar

1 clove garlic

4 peppercorns

1 clove

1 head of dill

or

½ teaspoon dill seed

In a saucepan boil for 5 minutes

2 quarts cider vinegar

1 cup pickling salt (often available as coarse Kosher salt)

Pour the hot liquid into the jars and fill to within ½" of the top. Make more vinegar-water-salt mixture if needed. Seal the jars by placing in a boiling water bath for 10 minutes. Let mellow at least a week before serving.

PURSLANE GUMBO

A good substantial half-wild stew. The purslane will thicken the stew slightly, as does the okra in the original recipe.

Melt in a heavy frying pan

3 tablespoons oil (bacon fat or cooking oil)

Add and sauté (gently fry) until golden brown on all sides

4 pounds of cut-up chicken

When tender, place on paper toweling to absorb excess fat. Melt an additional
- 3 tablespoons oil (bacon fat or cooking oil)

Add
- 2 onions (wild or domestic), chopped coarsely
- 4 cups purslane, chopped coarsely

Cook and stir 5 minutes. Add
- 1 quart canned tomatoes (or 4 fresh tomatoes and 3 cups water)
- 1 teaspoon salt

Cover and cook gently for 30 minutes Add
- 1 cup white or brown rice

Cook until rice is tender (20–40 minutes). Serve hot.

RASPBERRIES, BLACKBERRIES, AND THIMBLEBERRIES (Rubus spp.)

These berries are so good that many people prefer them just as they are collected from the bush. Besides the recipes given below, these berries can be substituted in the strawberry section in the "Bowle" and "Shortcake" recipes.

PLAIN BERRIES

Perhaps the best recipe of all.

Place in serving dishes
- wild berries, plain, washed, and unchilled

Serve with
- a pitcher of cream
- a bowl of powdered sugar
  or
- a touch of maple syrup

CHILLED BERRY SOUP

Combine in a blender
- 2 cups wild berries, washed and with stems removed
- 2 cups yogurt
- 2 cups buttermilk (or sour cream)
- 2 tablespoons lemon or lime juice
- 1 quart orange juice, freshly squeezed or frozen
- 1 tablespoon honey
- ¼ teaspoon cinnamon
- ⅛ teaspoon nutmeg

Chill and add just before serving
- a handful of whole wild berries, washed and with stems removed
- (optional) 2 tablespoons fresh mint, chopped

RASPBERRY, BLACKBERRY, OR THIMBLEBERRY JAM

Wash and remove stems from
- 2 quarts of wild berries

Place them in a mixing bowl and crush thoroughly with a potato masher or wooden spoon. Measure 5 cups of berries.

In a heavy large pan, place
- the 5 cups of berries
- 1 package of Sure-Jell fruit pectin

Mix well and bring to a full boil over high heat, stirring constantly. Immediately stir in
- 7 cups sugar

Return to a full boil and boil hard for 1 minute, stirring constantly. Remove from heat and let stand 2 minutes. Remove foam and ladle immediately into
- hot, sterilized jelly jars

Clean off the tops with a damp cloth and seal with
- paraffin, melted over hot water

FRUIT LEATHER

Place in a blender or food mill and blend throughly
- 4 cups ripe fruit, washed and stems removed
- 1 teaspoon honey
- 1 teaspoon fresh lemon juice
- ½ teaspoon cinnamon

Place the puréed fruit in a heavy saucepan and cook over very low heat, stirring constantly, until the mixture has a consistency of thick oatmeal. Spread the thickened fruit sauce in an 1/8" layer on cookie sheets. If weather is sunny, hot, and dry, place outside; if cool and/or humid, dry in a 140° oven with the door ajar a few inches. When completely dry (about 8–10 hours), roll in
   (optional) sugar
and roll into scrolls or tubes. Store in a cool, dry place.

RASPBERRY CHIFFON PIE

Prepare a pie crust as in the hickory nut section, under "Hickory Nut Pie" or a crumb crust as in the May apple section under "May Apple Chiffon Pie"

Wash, remove stems, and slice
   1½ cups raspberries
Place in a mixing bowl and cover with
   ½ cup sugar
Let stand ½ hour. In a medium saucepan mix
   1 envelope gelatine
   ¾ cup water
   1 tablespoon lemon juice, freshly squeezed
   ⅛ teaspoon salt
   ¼ cup sugar
Cook, stirring constantly, over low heat about 5 minutes, or until sugar dissolves. Cool slightly and add to the berry-sugar mixture. Chill until partially thickened. Beat until stiff and fold in
   2 egg whites
Pour the mixture into the pie crust or crumb crust and chill.

CHEESE CAKE WITH BERRY TOPPING

Make a crumb crust by combining in a mixing bowl
   1 cup zwieback crumbs or graham cracker crumbs
   ¼ cup butter or oleo, melted
   ¼ cup sugar
   ¼ teaspoon nutmeg
   ½ teaspoon cinnamon
Press firmly into the bottom of a 9" spring form pan.
Separate
   4 eggs
Beat the whites until stiff and add
   ¼ cup sugar
Set aside. In another mixing bowl, beat the yolks until thick. Add
   1 teaspoon vanilla
   1 cup sour cream
   ¾ cup sugar
   2 tablespoons flour
   ¼ teaspoon salt
   1 pound cream cheese, softened at room temperature
Fold in the beaten egg whites and pour into the crust. Bake until firm to the touch, about 1 hour. Chill. Serve with
   3 cups of wild berries, washed, stems removed and berries slightly crushed
         OR
Combine in a blender and spread over the cooled cheese cake
   3 cups of wild berries, washed, stems removed
   ¾ cup sugar
   1 tablespoon lemon juice, freshly squeezed

SHEEP SORREL
(*Rumex acetosella*)

Raw sorrel leaves are good simply washed, shredded, and added to lettuce, spinach, or potato salads.

SORREL PURÉE

Simple to make and a classic French accompaniment to fish, egg, or veal dishes.

In a medium saucepan, melt
   4 tablespoons butter or oleo

Add
>   1 large onion, thinly sliced
>   or
>   ¼ cup wild onions, chopped

Sauté until onion is almost tender. Add
>   1 quart of sorrel leaves, shredded

Cook, stirring constantly, until the leaves "melt" (cook down).
Add and heat almost to boiling
>   ½ cup milk or cream

Serve in a little pitcher as a sauce or pour over a main dish.

SORREL MAYONNAISE

Place in a blender
>   1 egg

Cover and blend at top speed for 30 seconds
Add
>   ¼ teaspoon dry mustard
>   ½ teaspoon salt
>   1 tablespoon lemon juice, freshly squeezed

Add slowly while blender is running
>   a scant cup salad oil
>   (safflower, sunflower or olive)
>   1 cup sorrel leaves, washed

Use in place of regular mayonnaise; excellent in sandwiches.

CREAM OF SORREL SOUP

This recipe was given to us by our horticulturalist-gourmet cook friend, Pat Pachuta.

Wash and cut into fine shreds
>   1 pound sorrel leaves

Set aside. In a medium saucepan, melt
>   ¼ cup butter or oleo

Add
>   ½ cup onion (wild or domestic) chopped

Sauté until the onion is lightly browned. Add the sorrel leaves and cook, stirring constantly, until the leaves "melt" (cook down).

Add
>   3 cups chicken broth (homemade, canned, or made from bouillon cubes)

Simmer for 5 minutes.
In a small bowl beat
>   2 egg yolks
>   1 cup heavy cream
>   ⅛ teaspoon tabasco sauce
>   ¼ teaspoon pepper, freshly ground
>   ¾ teaspoon salt

Add to simmering liquid and heat to just under a boil. Serve hot or chilled.

SORREL-BARLEY POTATO SOUP

Another excellent recipe from Pat Pachuta; it rapidly became a favorite at our botanical gatherings.

Combine in a large saucepan
>   10 cups water
>   ⅔ cup quick-cooking barley
>   2 pounds potatoes (3 large ones) peeled and cubed
>   2 teaspoons salt
>   ½ teaspoon ground allspice

Boil gently until tender but not mushy.
In a small skillet melt
>   ⅔ cup butter

Add and sauté until golden brown
>   1 large onion, thinly sliced
>   or
>   ¼ cup wild onions, sliced

To the barley mixture add
>   6 cups sorrel, washed and coarsely chopped

Boil 5 minutes, then add
>   the sautéed onions
>   1 cup cream (heavy cream makes a nice rich soup)

Simmer gently several minutes. Serve hot or cold.

SPICEBUSH (Lindera benzoin)

SPICEBUSH TEA

In a medium saucepan, place
- 1 cup spicebush twigs, broken or cut into pieces
- 2 quarts water

Bring to just under a boil and simmer gently for 15 minutes. Tea will be almost colorless. For more robust flavor and color, steep for ½ hour; add more hot water if it is too strong.
Serve with
- a pitcher of honey

SPICED SPICEBUSH TEA

In a medium saucepan, place
- 1 cup spicebush twigs, broken or cut into pieces
- 2 quarts water
- 3 whole allspice
- 3 whole cloves
- 1 4″ stick cinnamon

Steep 15 minutes, with the tea just under a boil.
Add
- ¼ cup brown sugar
- 1 tablespoon honey

Simmer until the sugar and honey dissolve, about 10 minutes.

SPICEBUSH JELLY

Serve this with meats, especially wild game.

In a large saucepan, mix
- 3 cups strong, cold spicebush tea
- 1 package Sure-Jell fruit pectin
- ½ teaspoon citric acid

Bring to a full boil and add
- 4 cups sugar

Return to a full, rolling boil and boil hard for 1 minute. Remove from heat. Let stand 2 minutes, then skim off foam. Pour into
- **sterilized jelly jars**

and seal with
- **paraffin, melted over hot water**

STRAWBERRIES (Fragaria virginiana)

MAI BOWLE

A festive German punch.

In a glass serving pitcher, place
- 2 cups wild strawberries, washed and hulled
- 2 tablespoons honey or sugar
- 2 tablespoons lemon juice
- ½ bottle dry white wine

Refrigerate for 2 hours or more. Add
- remaining ½ bottle of white wine
- 1 bottle Sekt or Champagne
- (optional) a glass of red wine for color and flavor

Serve chilled and topped with
- ½ cup fresh wild strawberries, washed and hulled

MAI BOWLE

A non-alcoholic version of the German punch.

In a glass serving pitcher, place
- 2 cups wild strawberries, washed and hulled
- 1 cup wild strawberries, washed and hulled and blended until smooth in a blender or put through a sieve or food mill
- 2 tablespoons honey or sugar
- 2 tablespoons lemon juice or lime juice
- 1 bottle white grape juice, tonic water, ginger ale, apple cider, or any sparkling fruit juices

Refrigerate for 2 hours or more. Add
- ½ cup fresh wild strawberries, washed and hulled

STRAWBERRY JAM

A delicious way to make a few berries go a long way.

Wash and hull
- 2 quarts of wild strawberries

Place them in a mixing bowl and crush thoroughly with a potato masher or wooden spoon. Measure 5 cups of berries.
In a heavy large pan, place
> the 5 cups of strawberry purée (smashed strawberries)
> 1 package of Sure-Jell fruit pectin

Mix well and bring to a full boil over high heat, stirring constantly. Immediately stir in
> 7 cups sugar

Return to a full boil and boil hard for 1 minute, stirring constantly. Remove from heat and let stand for 3 minutes. Remove foam and ladle immediately into
> hot jelly jars

Clean off the tops with a damp cloth and seal with
> paraffin, melted over hot water

WILD STRAWBERRY SHORTCAKE

To make the shortcake, combine in a mixing bowl
> 2 cups flour
> ¾ teaspoon salt
> 4 teaspoons baking powder

Cut in with pastry cutter or fingers
> 4 very heaping tablespoons white shortening

Add
> ¾ cup plus 1 tablespoon milk

Stir just until combined and toss on floured board gently for a few moments. Divide the dough in half and pat each into 9" rounds. Place one round in a pie pan and pour over it
> 2 tablespoons butter or oleo, melted

Place the other half of rolled dough on top of the first half and bake at 350° until tender and lightly browned, about 12 minutes.
Split carefully into the 2 original rounds.
To make the topping, crush together gently in a mixing bowl
> 1 quart of wild strawberries, washed and hulled
> 1 tablespoon honey or sugar

Taste for sweetness (add more honey or sugar if desired) and pour a third of this mixture over the lower biscuit round. Replace biscuit top and pour the remaining strawberry mixture over the whole shortcake. Serve with
> 1 cup heavy cream, unsweetened
> OR

Place in small bowl and whip until stiff peaks form
> 1 cup heavy cream
> 2 tablespoons honey or sugar
> ½ teaspoon vanilla

STRAWBERRY SHERBET

Wash and remove hulls from
> 2 quarts of wild strawberries

Force the berries through a sieve or purée in a food mill. In a mixing bowl combine
> the sieved berries
> 1½ cups sugar
> ¼ cup lemon juice, freshly squeezed

Beat several minutes until well blended. In a small bowl beat until soft peaks form
> 2 egg whites

Add to the strawberry mixture and freeze for 2 hours. Remove from freezer, beat until smooth and stir in
> 1 cup heavy cream

Freeze until solid. Serve plain or topped with
> ½ cup fresh wild strawberries, washed and hulled

STRAWBERRY LEAF TEA, FRESH

Combine in a large saucepan
> 1 small handful of fresh strawberry leaves (use flowers also, if they are in season)
> 2 quarts of cold water

Bring almost to a boil and simmer for 15

minutes. Strain out the leaves and flowers and serve with
   a pitcher of honey

STRAWBERRY LEAF TEA, DRIED

Dry in a single layer on newspaper, away from wind and bugs
   clean leaves of strawberries (flowers, too, if available)
Dry until crinkly dry, usually about 24 hours. Store in jars with a screw lid, away from heat and light. To make tea, place in a large saucepan
   1 small handful of dried leaves
   2½ quarts of cold water
Bring almost to a boil and simmer for 15 minutes. Strain out the leaves and flowers and serve with
   a pitcher of honey

SUMAC (Rhus spp.)

SUMAC LEMONADE

Collect the heads of sumac by snapping them off with fingers or by cutting with a knife or clippers. Fruit must be fully red and ripe. Discard any stems. Rinse well in cold water. Soak together in a pitcher or medium saucepan for 30 minutes
   6 heads of red sumac
   2 quarts of water
Stir the sumac heads with a wooden spoon to release their flavor. Pour the mixture through cheesecloth or a clean towel.
Heat in a small saucepan
   ¼ cup honey (may need more)
   ½ cup water
Stir to dissolve the honey and add to the sumac mixture. Mixture will be a light pink. Serve chilled.

SUMAC TEA

In a saucepan, bring to just under a boil
   4 heads of red sumac
   2 quarts water
Stir the sumac heads with a wooden spoon to release their flavor. Pour the mixture through cheesecloth or a clean towel. Return to the pan and add
   ¼ cup honey (may need more)
Stir until the honey dissolves. Serve warm. Color will be a dusky pink.

SUMAC JELLY

The short boiling time does not bother the delicate flavor.

Prepare a flavorful tea by either the "Sumac Lemonade" recipe or the "Sumac Tea" recipe. Measure and place in a large kettle
   7 cups sumac tea or lemonade
   1 box fruit pectin (such as Sure-Jell)
Bring to a full boil, stirring constantly. Add
   9 cups (4 pounds) of sugar
Return to a boil and boil hard one minute, stirring constantly. Remove from heat and allow to stand for 2 minutes. Skim off foam and ladle the jelly into
   hot, sterilized jelly jars
Cover with
   paraffin, melted over hot water

SUMAC SPICE

This tasty condiment is used in Middle Eastern cooking, where it flavors a variety of chicken, lamb, rice, and yogurt dishes.

Collect on a dry day
   2 quarts clean, fully ripe red sumac fruits
Place them on newspaper and let them dry completely, indoors or outdoors, about 12 hours. Separate the red berries

from the stems. Pound the fruits with a mortar and pestle, a wooden mallet, or pulverize in a blender. For every 2 tablespoons of powdered sumac, add
- 1 teaspoon dried thyme
- 1 teaspoon sesame seeds, lightly roasted in the oven

Store in a cool, dark, dry cupboard.

SUMAC CHICKEN

The following authentic Middle Eastern recipe was given to us by Mrs. Stanley Gex.

In a medium saucepan, boil until almost tender
- 4 chicken breasts
- water to cover

Remove chicken pieces and pat them dry. Split breasts in half and save the chicken broth. In a heavy frying pan, melt
- 4 tablespoons butter or oleo
- 1 tablespoon cooking oil

Add the chicken pieces and brown them over medium heat. Remove from frying pan and keep warm in a baking dish. In the frying pan, after the chicken pieces have all been browned, melt an additional
- 4 tablespoons butter or oleo

Add
- 4 onions (wild or domestic), thinly sliced

Sauté for 5 minutes. Add enough of the chicken broth to make a thin sauce. Set aside.
Split in half
- 4 small loaves of Italian or pita bread

Baste the inside of each loaf with
- melted butter

Place two pieces of chicken in each loaf. Season with
- a shake of salt
- a twist of pepper, freshly ground

Spread cooked onions and 2 tablespoons of the thin onion sauce over the chicken and top each loaf with
- 1 teaspoon sumac spice (see "Sumac Spice" recipe)

Bake in baking dish at 350° for 40 minutes.

WALNUTS AND BUTTERNUTS
(Juglans nigra and J. cinerea)

WALNUT CHICKEN

Cut into ½" thick pieces
- 1½ pounds chicken breast

Place in a mixing bowl and add
- 4 tablespoons soy sauce
- 1 tablespoon sherry
- 1½ tablespoons cornstarch
- ¼ teaspoon freshly ground pepper
- 1 egg white, slightly beaten

Marinate in refrigerator for ½ hour or more. Chop with a knife or pulverize in a blender
- ¾ cup walnuts

Drain chicken pieces and wipe off excess juice on paper toweling. Roll chicken pieces in the pulverized nuts. Heat in a heavy frying pan or a wok
- 5 tablespoons cooking oil

Add chicken and cook until golden brown, about 2 minutes on a side. Sprinkle with
- 2 tablespoons parsley

Serve with
- lemon wedges

WALNUT-APPLE SALAD

Combine in a serving bowl
- ¾ cup mayonnaise (see recipe below or use commercial mayonnaise)
- ½ cup walnuts, coarsely chopped
- 1 cup celery, diced
- 1 cup full-flavored apples, cored and chopped

To make mayonnaise, break into a blender
- 1 egg

Cover and blend ½ minute.
Add
> 1 tablespoon lemon juice or vinegar
> ¼ teaspoon dry mustard
> ½ teaspoon salt

Blend 15 seconds. With blender turned to high speed, drizzle in slowly
> about ¾ cup oil (olive or safflower oils are good)

until the mixture thickens.

SPICED NUTS

This recipe from Gloria Frankena is positive proof that neighbors are well worth having.

Beat until frothy in a medium sized mixing bowl
> 1 egg white
> 1 teaspoon water

Add
> ½ cup sugar
> ¼ teaspoon salt
> ½ teaspoon cinnamon
> ½ teaspoon nutmeg
> ¼ teaspoon cloves
> 1 pound walnuts or butternuts, shells removed

Place on greased baking sheet and bake 1 hour at 225°. Stir every 15 minutes, until the nuts are lightly browned.

WALNUT FUDGE PIE

A recipe from a wonderful cook and good friend, Cindy Edwards. Make pie crust as in the "Hickory Pie" recipe. Bake 4 minutes. Cool.

In the top of a double boiler, melt
> ¼ pound of butter or oleo
> 3 squares bitter chocolate

Cool slightly.
In a mixing bowl, combine
> ¾ cup walnuts or butternuts, broken into small pieces
> 4 eggs, slightly beaten
> 3 tablespoons light corn syrup
> 1½ cups sugar
> ¼ teaspoon salt
> ¼ cup milk
> 1 teaspoon vanilla
> the slightly cooled butter-chocolate mixture

Pour into the crust and bake at 450° for 10 minutes. Lower heat to 350° and bake for 30 minutes more or until the top is crusty and filling is set. Cool. Serve with whipped cream topping.

WHIPPED CREAM TOPPING

Whip in a small bowl until soft peaks form
> ½ pint whipping cream

Add
> 3 tablespoons sugar
> ½ teaspoon vanilla

Continue to beat until stiff peaks form. Spread topping over cooled pie or torte or serve separately in a small pitcher.

HUGUENOT TORTE

Another delicious recipe from Cindy Edwards.

Break into a medium mixing bowl
> 2 eggs

Beat them until thick and lemon-colored. Add and beat until thickened
> 1 cup plus 3 tablespoons sugar

Set aside. Sift together on wax paper
> ¼ cup flour
> 2½ teaspoons baking powder
> ¼ teaspoon salt

Add the flour mixture to the sugar mixture. Peel, core, and chop enough apples to make
> 1 cup apples

Add the apples to the mixing bowl along with
> 1 cup walnuts or butternuts, finely chopped
> 1 teaspoon vanilla

Blend gently and pour the batter into a well buttered baking dish (8" × 12"). Bake at 325° for about ½ hour. The top will be crunchy with a softer layer beneath. Cut in squares and serve with "Whipped Cream Topping" (see recipe above)

WATERCRESS
(Nasturtium officinale)

WATERCRESS SOUP

This soup delighted our class when made by one of our field assistants, Nancy Weintrub.

In a heavy frying pan melt
- 4 tablespoons butter or oleo

Add
- ½ cup wild or domestic onions, chopped

Sauté (fry gently) until onion is transparent.
Add
- 2 carrots, sliced thinly
- 2 potatoes, peeled and diced
- 8 cups chicken or vegetable stock (homemade, canned or made from bouillon cubes)

Blend well and boil gently until vegetables are just tender, about 15 minutes. In a separate pan, boil
- 6 cups of water

Add
- 2 cups of watercress, washed and chopped

Boil 3 minutes. Drain and stir watercress into the stock-vegetable mixture.
Add
- 1 teaspoon salt
- ½ teaspoon pepper, freshly ground

Pour into individual serving bowls and top each with
- a dollop of cream, whipped or sour (a dollop is a rounded tablespoonful)

WATERCRESS SANDWICH FILLING

Cream together in a small mixing bowl
- 6 ounces cream cheese, softened at room temperature
- ¼ cup heavy sour cream

Add
- 2 cups watercress leaves, washed and chopped
- ½ teaspoon salt
- ¼ teaspoon pepper, freshly ground

Blend well and serve with
- crackers or slices of whole wheat bread

WATERCRESS SPREAD

Cream
- ¼ pound butter or oleo, softened at room temperature
- 2 tablespoons watercress, washed and chopped
- 1 tablespoon parsley, chopped
- 1 tablespoon chives or wild onions, chopped
- ¼ teaspoon salt

Blend well and serve with
- crackers or slices of whole wheat bread

WATERCRESS SALAD DRESSING

Combine in a blender
- ½ cup watercress, washed
- ¼ cup salad oil (olive or safflower)
- 2 tablespoons vinegar or lemon juice, freshly squeezed
- 1 egg
- ¼ teaspoon salt
- ¼ teaspoon brown sugar or honey
- ¼ cup onion, wild or domestic

Blend thoroughly and chill. Serve over
- spinach, lettuce, or watercress leaves

WATERCRESS DUMPLINGS

Sift together
- 1 cup flour
- 2 teaspoons baking powder
- ½ teaspoon sugar
- ½ teaspoon salt

Cut in with pastry cutter or fingers
- 2 tablespoons butter or oleo

Add
- ½ cup milk
- 1 egg, well beaten
- ¾ cup watercress, washed and finely chopped

Pour by tablespoonfuls on
- stew or gravy or thickened soup

Cook, uncovered, for 10 minutes. Cover and cook 10 minutes longer.

WILD GINGER
(Asarum canadense)

WILD GINGER BARBECUED RIBS

Combine and simmer in a saucepan for 15 minutes
- 3 tablespoons wild ginger rhizomes, chopped
- 1 tablespoon honey
- 2 cloves of crushed garlic
- ¾ cup soy sauce
- ¼ cup wild or domestic onions, chopped finely
- (optional) 1 tablespoon sherry

Pour over
- spareribs or pork chops, cut up

Marinate several hours or overnight in refrigerator. Broil 15 minutes on each side in oven. Serve with
- lemon wedges

WILD GINGER FIELD-TRIP CHICKEN

In a heavy large frying pan combine and bring to a boil
- 2 tablespoons wild ginger rhizomes, scrubbed well and chopped
- ¼ cup wild or domestic onions, chopped
- ½ cup soy sauce
- 2 tablespoons honey
- 2 teaspoons Chinese five-spice powder
- (optional) ½ cup sherry

Add
- 4 pounds of chicken, cut into pieces

Cook until tender, 30–45 minutes depending on thickness of the chicken, stirring frequently. Serve hot or cold.

WILD GINGER CANDY

Clean and chop into 1" pieces
- 4 cups of wild ginger rhizomes

Place them in a saucepan and cover with
- cold water

Boil until the rhizomes are tender, about 1 hour.

Mix together
- ½ teaspoon cream of tartar
- 1 tablespoon cold water

Add
- 2 cups of sugar
- or
- 1⅛ cup honey

Combine all ingredients and boil gently for 20 minutes more. Drain and roll pieces in granulated sugar when cool.

GINGER SUNDAE SAUCE

Combine in a saucepan
- 2 tablespoons wild ginger rhizomes, cleaned and cut in small pieces
- 1 cup of sugar
- or
- ⅔ cup honey
- 1 cup of water

Boil gently for ½ hour or until it thickens a bit. Cool slightly, and add
- ½ teaspoon vanilla

Serve hot or cold over
- ice cream, mounded in individual dishes or in a large serving bowl

WILD RICE
(Zizania aquatica)

BOILED WILD RICE

Soak for 30 minutes
- 1 cup wild rice
- 4 cups cold water

Place the wild rice in a sieve and rinse well under running water. Drain well. Boil in a medium saucepan
- 3 cups water
- 1 teaspoon salt

Add the rice and boil until tender, about 30 minutes. Serve with
- 4 tablespoons butter or oleo, melted

MUSHROOM WILD RICE

Soak for 30 minutes
- 1 cup wild rice
- 4 cups cold water

Place the wild rice in a sieve and rinse well under running water. Drain well. Boil in a medium saucepan
- 3 cups water
- 1 teaspoon salt

Add the rice and boil until tender, about 30 minutes. Set aside. Melt in a heavy frying pan
- 4 tablespoons butter or oleo

Add
- ½ pound fresh mushrooms (wild edible or domestic) sliced
- ¼ cup onions (wild or domestic) chopped
- ¼ cup green pepper
- 2 tablespoons parsley
- ¼ teaspoon black pepper, freshly ground

Sauté over gentle heat for 8 minutes, stirring often. Combine with the cooked wild rice and heat thoroughly.

WILD RICE AND CHICKEN

Cook rice as in "Boiled Wild Rice" but do not top with butter. Instead place in a frying pan
- 4 tablespoons butter or oleo
- 1 tablespoon cooking oil

Add
- ½ cup onion (wild or domestic) chopped
- 1 pound of chicken livers or breast, thinly sliced

Sauté until just tender, about 10 minutes. Add
- 1 cup chicken stock (homemade, canned or made from bouillon)

Mix well and pour all ingredients including rice into a casserole and top with
- 3 tablespoons butter

Bake at 350° for 20 minutes.

WILD RICE CROQUETTES

Cook rice as in "Boiled Wild Rice" but do not top with butter. In a medium mixing bowl combine
- the cooked rice
- 4 egg yolks, beaten
- ½ teaspoon garlic, minced
- 1 teaspoon onion, minced
- 1 tablespoon parsley, finely chopped
- 1 tablespoon chives, finely chopped
- ½ teaspoon salt
- ¼ teaspoon black pepper, freshly ground

Chill and form into golf ball size pieces. Mix together
- 2 eggs, beaten
- ½ cup milk

Dip rice balls in the egg-milk mixture. Heat to almost smoking (390°) in a medium saucepan
- 1 quart cooking oil

Fry the rice balls until brown, 2–3 minutes.

WILD RICE PUFFS

Cook ½ recipe as in "Boiled Wild Rice" but do not top with butter. Set aside.
Bring to a boil in a small saucepan

½ cup water
¼ cup butter or oleo
½ teaspoon salt

Remove from heat and add

½ cup flour

Return to heat, stirring constantly, until mixture pulls away from the side of the pan. Cool slightly, then add, one at a time

2 eggs

Beat well after each addition and add

1 tablespoon butter or oleo
the wild rice

Heat in a heavy saucepan until very hot

4 cups oil

Drop the rice mixture by spoonfuls into the hot fat. They will turn over when done on the bottom. Drain and serve as an accompaniment to the main course.

MINNESOTA WILD RICE SOUP

In a large frying pan, melt

3 tablespoons butter or oleo
1 tablespoon cooking oil

Add

½ cup onions (wild or domestic), thinly sliced
¼ pound mushrooms (domestic or properly identified edible wild fungi), thinly sliced

Sauté 5 minutes, stirring often. Add

¼ cup flour

Stir until smooth, about 5 more minutes. Add

1½ quarts chicken broth (homemade, canned or made from bouillon cubes)

Cook, stirring often for 10 minutes. Add

1½ cups cooked wild rice (see "Boiled Wild Rice" recipe)
1 cup light cream
(optional) ¼ cup sherry

Heat thoroughly, but do not boil. Serve hot, topped with

¼ cup parsley, chopped
    or
¼ cup chives, chopped

WINTERGREEN
(Gaultheria procumbens)

WINTERGREEN TEA

Beat, cut, or mix in a blender

2 cups wintergreen leaves (and ripe, red fruits, if available)
2 quarts cold water

In a large saucepan, bring the mixture almost to a boil and simmer for 15 minutes. Serve hot with

a pitcher of honey

WINTERGREEN SALAD DRESSING

Heat in a small pan until the mixture boils

½ cup vinegar
1 tablespoon honey
¼ teaspoon salt
3 tablespoons ripe, red wintergreen fruits, chopped

Chill, then pour over

2 cups of raw spinach, or lamb's quarters, washed and torn gently into pieces
2 cups lettuce, washed and torn gently into pieces
3 tablespoons additional chopped wintergreen fruits

WINTERGREEN JELLY

Crush or chop finely

2½ cups packed wintergreen leaves (fruits, too, if available)

In a saucepan mix

the chopped wintergreen leaves
3½ cups water

Bring the mixture to a boil; remove from heat and let stand for 15 minutes. Pour through cheesecloth or clean pillowcase. Discard the leaves and ignore the insipid color. Measure 3 cups of the above wintergreen infusion (liquid) and add to a large kettle with

1 box Sure-Jell fruit pectin

Bring to a full boil stirring constantly. At once add

4 cups (1¾ pounds) sugar

Return to a boil and boil hard for 1 minute, stirring constantly. Remove from heat. Let stand 2 minutes, skim off foam and pour into

hot, sterilized jelly jars

Clean off tops with a damp cloth and cover with

paraffin, melted over hot water

WINTERGREEN ICE CREAM

Mix and heat almost to boiling in a heavy large pan (or the top of a double boiler placed over boiling water)

3 cups strong wintergreen tea
8 cups cold water
2 cups skim milk powder

Mix in a separate bowl

2 cups sugar
6 tablespoons flour
2 teaspoons salt

Add the sugar mixture gradually to the hot milk mixture. Heat, stirring constantly, until sugar dissolves, about 8 minutes. Remove from heat and stir 2 tablespoons of the hot liquid into a small bowl with

3 eggs, beaten

Pour egg mixture back into the hot milk mixture. Cook, stirring constantly, until mixture coats a spoon (leaves a thin film on a spoon dipped into the liquid). Remove from heat. Mix together in a small bowl

2 envelopes unflavored gelatine
½ cup cold water

Add the gelatine mixture to the hot liquid and stir. Cool, then freeze for 2 hours. Remove the ice cream and stir to fluff it up and mellow the texture. Return to freezer and freeze hard.

EDIBLE WILD PLANTS

RECIPE LIST
ACCORDING TO TYPES

APPETIZERS
Hazelnut Appetizer 85
Jerusalem Artichoke Appetizer
  with Dip 91
Purslane Dip, Raw 107

BEVERAGES
Blueberry Juice, Norwegian
  Style 76
Cranberry Juice 80
Elder Flower Tea 82
Elderberry Juice, Mulled 82
Grape Juice 83
High Bush Cranberry Juice 89
Japanese Knotweed Juice 90
Mai Bowle, Alcoholic 111
Mai Bowle, Non-alcoholic 111
May Apple Juice 95
Mint Breakfast Drink 98
Mint Tea 98
New Jersey Tea, Dried 102
New Jersey Tea, Fresh 102
New Jersey Tea, Spiced 102
Pawpaw Punch, Tropical 104
Spicebush Tea 111
Spicebush Tea, Spiced 111
Strawberry Leaf Tea, Dried 113
Strawberry Leaf Tea, Fresh 112
Sumac Lemonade 113
Sumac Tea 113
Wintergreen Tea 119

BREADS AND GRAINS
Blueberry Buckle 77
Blueberry Muffins 76
Blueberry Pancakes 77
Cranberry-Nut Bread 80
Jerusalem Artichoke Pancakes ... 91
Maple Syrup and Biscuits 94
Mushroom Wild Rice 118
Pawpaw Bread 105
Watercress Dumplings 117
Wild Rice, Boiled 118
Wild Rice Croquettes 118
Wild Rice Puffs 118

CAKES AND FROSTINGS
Apple-Hickory Nut Squares 87

Cat-tail Pollen Poundcake 78
Cheesecake with Berry Topping . 109
Hazelnut Cake, Jan Bruce's 86
Hazelnut Caramel Frosting 87
May Apple Hummingbird Cake ... 96

DESSERTS (see also cake, ice creams, and pies)
Berries, Plain 108
Blueberry Buckle 77
Caramel Pralines 88
Cream Puffs 89
Elder Flower Fritters 82
Fruit Leather 108
Ginger Sundae Sauce 117
Hazelnut Cookies 86
Hazelnut Soufflé 86
Huguenot Torte 115
Maple Syrup 94
Maple Syrup Fruit Topping 94
Mulberry Sauce 99
Nuts, Spiced 115
Pawpaw Pudding 105
Pawpaw Yogurt 104
Strawberry Shortcake, Wild 112
Whipped Cream Topping 115
Wild Ginger Candy 117

ICE CREAM/SHERBETS
Cranberry Sherbet 80
Elder Flower Sherbet 82
Ginger Sundae Sauce 117
Maple Walnut Ice Cream 94
May Apple Ice Cream 96
Pawpaw Yogurt 104
Strawberry Sherbet 112
Wintergreen Ice Cream 120

JAMS/JELLIES
Blackberry Jam 108
Blueberry Jam 76
Elderberry Jelly 83
Grape Jelly 85
High Bush Cranberry Jelly 89
May Apple Marmalade 95
Mint Jelly 98
Mulberry Jam 99

Raspberry Jam 108
Spicebush Jelly 111
Strawberry Jam 111
Sumac Jelly 113
Thimbleberry Jam 108
Wintergreen Jelly 119

MAIN DISHES
Asparagus Frittata 75
Asparagus with Chicken 75
Asparagus with Tofu 75
Nettle Yorkshire Pudding 101
Nettles in Greek Filo 101
Lamb's Quarters Quiche 93
Lamb's Quarters Under a Crust .. 93
Mint Chicken 99
Mint Tabouli 98
Mushroom Wild Rice 118
Sumac Chicken 114
Walnut Chicken 114
Wild Ginger Barbecued Ribs 117
Wild Ginger Field Trip Chicken . 117
Wild Rice and Chicken 118

MEDICINES
Magic Chickweed Potion 79
Old Gypsy Cure 83

PIES
Blueberry Pie 76
Elderberry-Apple Crumb Pie 83
Hickory Nut Pie 88
High Bush Cranberry Pie 89
Japanese Knotweed Pie 90
May Apple Chiffon Pie 95
Pawpaw Pie 105
Raspberry Chiffon Pie 109
Walnut Fudge Pie 115

PRESERVES
Cat-tail Shoots, Pickled 78
Grape Leaf Preservation 84
Jerusalem Artichoke Pickles 91
Milkweed Pods, Dilly 97
Milkweed Pods, Pickled 97
Purslane Dills 107
Sumac Spice 113

SALADS/DRESSINGS
Asparagus Salad, Chinese 75
Austrian Salad 107

Chickweed-Carrot Salad 79
Chickweed Wilted Salad 79
Dandelion Crowns, Marinated 81
Fiddleheads, Marinated 104
Hazelnut-Cucumber Salad 86
Hickory Nut Dressing 87
Japanese Knotweed Fruit
  Salad Dressing 90
Jerusalem Artichoke Salad 92
Maple Syrup 94
Mint Tabouli 98
Sorrel Mayonnaise 110
Walnut-Apple Salad 114
Watercress Sandwich Filling..... 116
Watercress Spread 116
Wintergreen Salad Dressing 119

SOUPS
Berry Soup, Chilled 108
Chickweed Hot and Sour Soup ... 78
Fiddlehead Soup 104
Lamb's Quarters, Cheese Soup
  with 92
Mulberry Soup 99
Nettle-Chicken Soup 100
Nettle-Leek Soup................ 101
Nut Soup, Cream of............. 87
Pokeweed Cheese Soup 106
Purslane Gumbo 107
Ramp Soup, Traditional 103
Sorrel-Barley-Potato Soup 110
Sorrel Soup, Cream of 110
Watercress Soup 116
Wild Onion Soup, French Style . 103
Wild Rice Soup, Minnesota 119

VEGETABLES
Asparagus, Country Style 75
Cat-tail Spikes, Boiled 78
Cat-tails Oriental 77
Dandelions, Boiled 81
Dandelions Oriental 82
Dandelions, Sweet and Sour 81
Fiddleheads, Marinated 104
Fiddleheads with Hollandaise
  Sauce 104
Grape Leaves, Stuffed 84
Ground Nuts, Deep Fried 85
Ground Nuts, Deviled 85
Ground Nuts, Sautéed 85
Japanese Knotweed, Boiled 90

Jerusalem Artichokes, Boiled 91
Lamb's Quarters, Boiled 92
Milkweed, General Processing 96
Milkweed Tempura 97
Milkweed with a Sauce of
  Milkweed 97
Nettle Soufflé 100
Nettle Yorkshire Pudding 101
Nettles, Boiled 100
Onions in Cream Sauce 103
Onions, Sautéed 102
Ostrich Fern, Boiled 103
Pokeweed au Gratin 106
Pokeweed, Boiled 105
Pokeweed, Pennsylvania Dutch .. 106
Sorrel Purée 109

COMPLETE INDEX

Acer spp. 29
Allium spp. 40
Apios americana 17
Apple-Hickory Nut Squares 87
Asarum canadense 58
Asclepias syriaca 31
Asimina triloba 42
Asparagus 5
Asparagus, Country Style 75
Asparagus Frittata 75
Asparagus officinalis 5
Asparagus Salad, Chinese 75
Asparagus with Chicken 75
Asparagus with Tofu 75
Austrian Salad 107

Beebalm 33
Berries, Plain 108
Berry Soup, Chilled 108
Berry Topping for Cheesecake ... 109
Blackberries 46
Blackberry Jam 108
Blueberries 5
Blueberry Buckle 77
Blueberry Jam 76
Blueberry Juice, Norwegian 76
Blueberry Muffins 76
Blueberry Pancakes 77
Blueberry Pie 76
Bracken Fern 8
Butternuts 56

Caramel Pralines 88
Carya ovalis and *C. ovata* 20
Catnip 33
Cat-tail Pollen Poundcake 78
Cat-tail Shoots, Pickled 78
Cat-tail Spikes, Boiled 78
Cat-tails 8
Cat-tails Oriental 77
Ceanothus americanus 37
Cheesecake with Berry Topping .. 109
Cheese Soup with Lamb's
    Quarters 92
Chenopodium album 26
Chickweed 10
Chickweed-Carrot Salad 79
Chickweed Hot and Sour Soup ... 78
Chickweed Potion, Magic 79

Chickweed, Wilted Salad 79
Corylus americana and
    C. cornuta 20
Cranberries 12
Cranberry Juice 80
Cranberry-Nut Bread 80
Cranberry Pudding 80
Cranberry Sherbet 80
Cream Puffs 89

Dandelion 13
Dandelion Crowns, Marinated 81
Dandelions, Boiled 81
Dandelions Oriental 82
Dandelions, Sweet and Sour 81

Elderberry 15
Elderberry-Apple Crumb Pie 83
Elderberry Jelly 83
Elderberry Juice, Mulled 82
Elder Flower Fritters 82
Elder Flower Sherbet 82
Elder Flower Tea 82

Fiddlehead Soup 104
Fiddleheads (see also Ostrich
    Fern) 40
Fiddleheads, Marinated 104
Fiddleheads with Hollandaise
    Sauce 104
Fragaria virginiana 53
Fruit Leather 108

Gaultheria procumbens 61
Ginger Sundae Sauce (see also Wild
    Ginger) 117
Grape Jelly 85
Grape Juice 83
Grape Leaf Preservation 84
Grape Leaves, Stuffed 84
Grapes 15
Ground Nuts 17
Ground Nuts, Deep Fried 85
Ground Nuts, Deviled 85
Ground Nuts, Sautéed 85

Hazelnut Appetizers 85
Hazelnut Cake, Jan Bruce's 86
Hazelnut Caramel Frosting 87

EDIBLE WILD PLANTS

Hazelnut Cookies 86
Hazelnut-Cucumber Salad 86
Hazelnut Soufflé 86
Hazelnuts 20
Helianthus tuberosus 24
Hickory Nut Dressing 87
Hickory Nut Pie 88
Hickory Nuts 20
High Bush Cranberries 22
High Bush Cranberry Jelly 89
High Bush Cranberry Juice 89
High Bush Cranberry Pie 89
Huguenot Torte 115

Japanese Knotweed 24
Japanese Knotweed, Boiled 90
Japanese Knotweed Fruit Salad
  Dressing 90
Japanese Knotweed Juice 90
Japanese Knotweed Pie, Deep
  Dish 90
Jerusalem Artichoke Appetizer 91
Jerusalem Artichoke Pancakes 91
Jerusalem Artichoke Pickles 91
Jerusalem Artichoke Salad 92
Jerusalem Artichokes, Boiled 91
Lamb's Quarters 26
Lamb's Quarters, Boiled 92
Lamb's Quarters in Cheese Soup .. 92
Lamb's Quarters Quiche 93
Lamb's Quarters Under a Crust ... 93
Lindera benzoin 51

Magic Chickweed Potion 79
Mai Bowle, Alcoholic 111
Mai Bowle, Non-alcoholic 111
Maple 29
Maple Syrup 94
Maple Syrup and Biscuits 94
Maple Syrup Fruit Topping 94
Maple Walnut Ice Cream 94
Matteuccia struthiopteris 40
May apple 29
May Apple Chiffon Pie 95
May Apple Hummingbird Cake ... 96
May Apple Ice Cream 96
May Apple Juice 95
May Apple Marmalade 95
Mentha spp. 33
Milkweed 31
Milkweed, General Processing 96

Milkweed Pods, Dilly 97
Milkweed Pods, Pickled 97
Milkweed Tempura 97
Milkweed with a Sauce of
  Milkweed 97
Mint 33
Mint Breakfast Drink 98
Mint Chicken 99
Mint Jelly 98
Mint Tabouli 98
Mint Tea 98
Monarda spp. 33
Morus alba 35
Mulberry 35
Mulberry Ice Cream, Doug's 100
Mulberry Jam 99
Mulberry Sauce 99
Mulberry Soup 99
Mushroom Wild Rice 118

Nasturtium officinale 56
Nepeta cataria 33
Nettle-Chicken Soup 100
Nettle-Leek Soup 101
Nettle Soufflé 100
Nettle Yorkshire Pudding 101
Nettles 36
Nettles, Boiled 100
Nettles in Greek Filo 101
New Jersey Tea 37
New Jersey Tea, Dried 102
New Jersey Tea, Fresh 102
New Jersey Tea, Spiced 102
Nut Soup, Cream of 87
Nuts, Spiced 115

Old Gypsy Cure 83
Onions 40
Onions in Cream Sauce 103
Onions, Sautéed 102
Ostrich Fern (see also
  Fiddleheads) 40
Ostrich Fern, Boiled 103

Pawpaw 42
Pawpaw Bread 105
Pawpaw Pie 105
Pawpaw Pudding 105
Pawpaw Punch, Tropical 104
Pawpaw Yogurt 104
Phytolacca americana 44

EDIBLE WILD PLANTS

Podophyllum peltatum 29
Pokeweed 44
Pokeweed au Gratin 106
Pokeweed, Boiled 105
Pokeweed Cheese Soup 106
Pokeweed, Pennsylvania Dutch .. 106
Polygonum cuspidatum 24
Portulaca oleracea 45
Pteridium aquilinum 8
Purslane 45
Purslane Dills 107
Purslane Gumbo 107
Purslane Dip, Raw 107

Ramp Soup, Traditional 103
Raspberries 46
Raspberry Chiffon Pie 109
Raspberry Jam 108
Rhus spp. 53
Rubus spp. 46
Rumex acetosella 50
Sambucus canadensis 15
Sassafras 48
Sassafras albidum 48
Sheep Sorrel 50
Sorrel-Barley-Potato Soup 110
Sorrel Mayonnaise 110
Sorrel Purée 109
Sorrel Soup, Cream of 110
Spicebush 51
Spicebush Jelly 111
Spicebush Tea 111
Spicebush Tea, Spiced 111
Stellaria media 10
Strawberries 53
Strawberry Jam 111
Strawberry Leaf Tea, Dried 113
Strawberry Leaf Tea, Fresh 112
Strawberry Sherbet 112
Strawberry Shortcake, Wild 112
Sumac 53
Sumac Chicken 114
Sumac Jelly 113
Sumac Lemonade 113
Sumac Spice 113

Sumac Tea 113

Taraxacum officinale 13
Thimbleberries 46
Thimbleberry Jam 108
Typha angustifolia and *T. latifolia* .. 8

Urtica dioica 36

Vaccinium angustifolium and *V. corymbosum* 5
Vaccinium macrocarpon and *V. oxycoccos* 12
Viburnum trilobum 22
Vitis spp. 15

Walnut-Apple Salad 114
Walnut Chicken 114
Walnut Fudge Pie 115
Walnuts 56
Watercress 56
Watercress Dumplings 117
Watercress Salad Dressing 116
Watercress Sandwich Filling ... 116
Watercress Soup 116
Watercress Spread 116
Whipped Cream Topping 115
Wild Ginger (see also Ginger) ... 58
Wild Ginger Barbecued Ribs ... 117
Wild Ginger Candy 117
Wild Ginger Field Trip Chicken .. 117
Wild Onion Soup, French Style .. 103
Wild Rice 59
Wild Rice and Chicken 118
Wild Rice, Boiled 118
Wild Rice Croquettes 118
Wild Rice Puffs 118
Wild Rice Soup, Minnesota 119
Wintergreen 61
Wintergreen Ice Cream 120
Wintergreen Jelly 119
Wintergreen Salad Dressing 119
Wintergreen Tea 119

Zizania aquatica 59